WITCH**CRAFT**
A HISTORY

P.G. Maxwell-Stuart is Lecturer in History at the University of St Andrews. His other books include *Witch Hunters: Professional Prickers, Unwitchers & Witch-Finders of the Renaissance* and *Wizards: A History*.

WITCHCRAFT
A HISTORY

P. G. MAXWELL-STUART

TEMPUS

Cover illustration: *Scène de sorcellerie* by Léonard Defrance, eighteenth century, courtesy of Musée de l'Art wallon de la ville de Liège.

First published 2000
This edition first published 2004

Tempus Publishing Limited
The Mill, Brimscombe Port,
Stroud, Gloucestershire, GL5 2QG
www.tempus-publishing.com

British Library Cataloguing in Publication Data.
A catalogue record for this book is available from the British Library.

ISBN 0 7524 2966 3

Typesetting and origination by Tempus Publishing Limited
Printed in Great Britain by Midway Colour Print, Wiltshire.

CONTENTS

PREFACE

Witchcraft is not an easy subject to write about, partly because the word itself is difficult to define. Attempts have been made, based on anthropological studies of non-European peoples, to distinguish between witchcraft as a preternatural power inborn in an individual and inherited from parents and grandparents, and sorcery as a set of magical techniques which may be taught and therefore learned. Such a distinction, however, is difficult to uphold in the context of Western European witchcraft, especially that relating to the medieval and early modern periods which constitute the era most commonly associated with both magic and witchcraft by Westerners.

It is easier, in fact, to suggest that witchcraft is what a witch does, and a witch is someone designated as such according to the legislation and communal beliefs of her or his particular region during the period of her or his lifetime. For although theologians and lawyers developed a working theory of witchcraft during the fifteenth century, which then lasted, with modifications, throughout the sixteenth and seventeenth centuries, the magical crimes of which someone might be accused varied, sometimes considerably, from place to place and from time to time.

What is more, the English words 'witch' and 'witchcraft' give a false impression of what magical operators were doing, since they tend to imply a uniformity of perception and practice from one end of Europe to another at any given time. But the extraordinarily varied vocabulary applied to these people and to what they were doing indicates an almost complete lack of uniformity outwith the confines of theological or legal treatises. The one point on which everyone was agreed was that certain magical acts by these operators were undesirable to the point of criminality, although the exact nature of those acts and the stage at which they reached a degree of criminality sufficient to provoke others into lodging a complaint before a court differed from time to time and from place to place. Defining 'witch' and 'witchcraft' thus runs the risk of turning into little more than a game of semantics.

I have not attempted to include witchcraft from parts of the world other than Western Europe and Central and North America. This is partly because inclusion of other witchcrafts would stretch the limits of this book beyond what is practicable, and partly because those other witchcrafts have little in common with the type long prevalent in Europe and in consequence deserve their own careful treatment rather than a brief, perhaps misleading summary. This is not to say, of course, that a comparison between other witchcrafts and the European variety would not be fruitful. But because, in spite of appearances to the contrary, we still have a great deal to learn about European witchcraft, the time is perhaps not yet ripe to undertake a comparison which would be useful and informative.

The translations in this book are my own with the following exceptions: (i) quotations from the Bible, which are given in the Authorized Version; (ii) quotations from the *Malleus Maleficarum*, for which I have used Montague Summers's translation; and (iii) the extract from Cazotte's *Le diable amoureux*, which appears in the English version of 1798.

I

'Witches' in Greece and Rome

In 1599, the internationally renowned Jesuit scholar Martín Del Rio published the first instalment of a huge work on all aspects of magic and the other occult sciences. In it, he included a description of how witches got to their meeting, the Sabbat, and what they did there once they had arrived. They fly, he said, on a staff of some kind, which they first smear with an ointment made from the fat of dead children, or they are carried on the back of an animal such as a goat. After they are set down, they see an evil spirit enthroned in their midst, whom they honour first by adopting various unnatural postures and then with a kiss upon his anus. Next, they mock the Mass and other Catholic ceremonies and then sit down to a meal, each one of them masked or veiled and attended by an evil spirit. After the meal, the whole company will dance and fall to perverse forms of copulation, following which every individual gives an account of his or her acts of wickedness since the last Sabbat, receiving savage physical punishment if the presiding spirit considers their actions not vile enough. Finally, they are given magical powders to assist their evil-doing in future, and make their way home, either on foot or in the same preternatural fashion by which they arrived.

This account, built up from a multitude of details Del Rio had come across in his extensive reading, will be familiar to modern readers, and may well constitute their immediate association with the word 'witch'. It is clear, however, that no such witches existed in the worlds of Greece and Rome. To be sure, it is common custom to use the word 'witch' in connection with their magical practitioners, but a witch, as conceived by Western historical record, is essentially a late medieval and early modern construct, dependent upon the particular manifestations of the Christian faith during those periods. So translating the various Greek and Roman words for magicians, diviners, necromancers, and so forth as 'witch' is both misleading and inaccurate. Nevertheless, certain ideas about magical workers, as well as the specialized vocabulary used to describe them, were passed on from the ancient to the medieval world, and in consequence any description of the Western witch must begin with that earlier period during which, strictly speaking, she or he did not exist.

The first-century AD Roman encyclopaedist Pliny the Elder advanced the notion that magic arose first from medicine and then went on to embrace religion and astrology.[1] Pliny thus saw magic as a practical art, alternative or complementary to the purely natural skills of the physician or herbalist. It was also, however, an art which relied on lines of communication to powers other than human to bring about ends which might otherwise not be obtainable. It is easy to see that this extension into the realms of preternature which the state religion would consider particularly its own would be likely to bring with it the possibility of conflict between magic and officially approved religious practice. Users of magic might seek to contact divinities on the fringe of the state cultus, or to manipulate the state's gods and goddesses for private ends. The Roman poet Lucan asked the obvious questions:

> What kind of physical distress do these incantations and herbs cause to celestial beings, which makes them do as they are told and be afraid to treat them with scorn? What is the business-arrangement, what is the pact by which [magicians] put the gods under an obligation to them? Are the gods forced to obey them, or do they obey because it gives them pleasure to do so? Are the gods rewarded by some kind of reciprocal relationship no one else knows about, or have they been prevailed upon by threats which no one else hears?
>
> *Bellum Civile* 6.492-6

These questions contain the seeds of the future debate about witches and their powers which both Catholic and Protestant theologians were to raise in their demonologies. Can Satan and his evil spirits really be compelled by mere humans to cooperate in magical operations, or does Satan just pretend to assist for the time being, with a view to seducing the magical operator further and further into sin? Is there a pact between the magician and the evil spirit? (This was a question which lay at the very heart of medieval and early modern attitudes to those who practised magic.) Does the relationship between magician and evil spirit involve idolatrous worship by the human? If so, has not he or she abandoned God and reverted to paganism or diabolism? No wonder, then, that the state (and in Christian times, the Church) took an active and often hostile interest in the activities of magical operators. Friction between official and unofficial cultus could easily become irritating and even intolerable. After all, attempts to foretell the future from the stars or from a variety of other divinatory instruments might take on an unwelcome political aspect, depending on whose future was being sought and who was doing the seeking. Even magical cures carried an element of danger should the patient not recover. Thus, in as far as magic (in any of its aspects) had the potential of coming into conflict with officially approved religion, medicine or divination, its practitioners were always likely to be regarded askance, in spite of the fact that there was always a great demand for their services and that this demand might also be made by those who were in a social or political position to inflict upon magicians and diviners the full penalties of legal or religious disapproval.

One should not be tempted to argue from this, however, that magical practitioners were necessarily 'marginalized'. Their inferior or alien status belonged, rather, to the self-regarding, self-appointed exclusivity of certain influential people. The fact is that in Athens and Rome (home to so many of the writers from whom we derive our information), both politics and state cultus were in the hands of a minority, that is to say, men who were citizens. Official views on any given subject therefore tended to reflect the opinions of this elite. By their definition, women, non-citizen males and foreigners fell outwith this privileged category, and in consequence official disapproval or prosecution of magic may be seen as an attempt to preserve the value and status of approved state religion, conventional medicine and official divination. Practice of illicit or unapproved magic would thus inevitably be associated with women, non-citizen males or foreigners (not to mention slaves), and such association would, itself, distance magic from the official cultus and diminish its worth in the eyes of those who, for whatever reason, were attached to the state-approved ways of managing religion, medicine, divination and any of their related activities.

The point may be illustrated from a passage by the historian Dio Cassius:

> Divination is necessary, to be sure, and one should certainly appoint people to divine the will of the gods from sacrifices and by observing the flights of birds, so that anyone who wishes to do so may frequent them and consult them about anything. But it is preferable that there be no such people as workers of magic, because although they sometimes speak the truth, people of that kind much more frequently tell lies and stir up many to make a revolution.
>
> Dio Cassius 52.36.3

Not surprisingly, these words are put in the mouth of a politician. They encapsulate official misgiving that unregulated occult activity may have dire consequences for the continued smooth running of society along state-approved, dirigiste lines, and that the state's disapproval could in practice be severe can be seen from the wholesale expulsion of astrologers and necromancers from Rome in 33 BC[2], and that it might go as far as what would later emotively be called a 'witch hunt' is shown by two extraordinary incidents of 184-183 and 180-179 BC, when large numbers of people (the historian Livy records, though with reservations, 2,000 and 3,000), were executed on charges of using *veneficia*, magic in some form or another, which was intended to do harm or even to kill.[3]

❦

But of what activities, precisely, was the state so nervous? Magical operators claimed to be able to control and direct love or sexual passion, cure physical ailments, counteract the effects of sorcery or inborn magic such as the evil eye, foretell the future, alienate crops and control the weather, or work preternatural harm upon other people, and it is useful to see what impression of Greek and Roman magicians is conveyed by surviving records.

The characteristic love-spell sought to do two things: to bind and to allure. 'Rouse yourself for me,' says one spell, addressing a small, clay female figure,

> 'and go into every place, into every quarter, into every house. Bind Ptolemais, the daughter of Horigenes. Bring her to me. Make her unable to eat or drink till she comes to me, and do not let her make love to any other man except me. Drag her by the hair, by the guts, until she does not keep me at a distance, and until I make her obedient to me for the rest of my life, loving me, desiring me, and telling me what she is thinking'.

Adapted from *Supplementum Magicum* 47.19-27

'Get hold of Euphemia', says another,

> 'and bring her to me, mad with desire for me. Bind her with strong chains made of adamantine so that she cannot escape because she loves me so much. Do not let her eat, drink, sleep, joke, or laugh, and make her abandon her father, mother, brothers, sisters, and come to me'.

Adapted from *Supplementum Magicum* 45

The violence of both is remarkable, the women against whom they are directed seeming to resemble hypnotized insects, drawn to a spider's web and stored there as future meals. It is a violence further illustrated by the various devices which were often used as accompaniments to these spells. Aphrodite, goddess of love and passion, for example, was said to have introduced human beings to the method whereby a wryneck was tied to the four spokes of a wheel which was then whirled round and round while an incantation was chanted.[4] Another involved manufacturing wax images in postures of domination and submission, and inserting several pins into parts of the female figure, much as one would if one wished to curse or otherwise harm rather than constrain and compel to passion, while a third used *pharmaka*, an ambiguous word referring (among other things) to physical substances such as roots or herbs or bark made up into some kind of potion. This method, as one may readily imagine, could sometimes prove fatal. A fifth-century BC court case relates the following incident. A man called Philoneus wanted to divest himself of his mistress. She, hoping to restore his love to its former state, was advised by another woman to slip a *pharmakon* into his drink, but had the unfortunate idea that if she gave Philoneus a larger dose than that which had been prescribed, his resulting love would turn out to be all the greater. The increased dosage, however, proved fatal, not only to Philoneus but also to another man who drank from the same wine-bowl, and in consequence the mistress was arrested, tried for murder, found guilty, and executed.[5]

There could be, however, a subversive side to erotic magic – the malevolent wish to prevent rather than attract sexual intercourse – and this can be seen in spells which reverse the notion of binding from its positive aspect of permanent attraction to the negative one of impotence or psychological castration. Ovid, for example, laments that on one particular occasion, in spite of his lover's beauty and lustfulness, he found himself unable to have intercourse with her and wonders, 'Surely it cannot be that my body has been bewitched and is now enfeebled because of a magical potion/spell [*venenum*]? Surely I am not the wretched victim of a malevolent incantation and noxious herbs? Or has a worker of harmful magic [*saga*] embedded my name in an image made from bright red wax, and thrust thin pins into the middle of its liver?'[6] An anonymous first-century BC encyclopaedia of amulets, *Cyranides*, gives instructions for one which will render a man unable to perform the sex act with a woman. The maker is to engrave upon obsidian a castrated man with his genitals beside his feet. The stone is then to be placed in a flat golden box which, in turn, is sewn into an embroidered belt made of falcon-sinew. Any male who touches this belt will immediately become impotent. In seeking to unbind the woman's dress, he will become bound himself.

When it comes to curing illness, remedies often consisted of the administration of some kind of medicine accompanied by incantations, or the wearing of an amulet specially prepared for the occasion. Pliny the Elder gives examples of all these in Book 30 of his *Naturalis Historia*, which consists of information drawn from both non-Roman and Roman sources. The former he tends to dismiss as worthless and superstitious; the latter he records without comment or accepts as valid. These magical cures fall into roughly two categories. One records remedies which do not overtly depend upon preternatural power for their efficacy. Thus, toothache can be relieved by cooking earthworms in oil which is then poured into the ear on the side where the pain is occurring[7]; livid spots and bruises are treated with thin slices of hot rams' or sheep's lungs, or with pigeon's dung[8]; eating weasel meat is good for scrofula[9]; and diarrhoea is checked by pounding a snail, shell and all, soaking it in wine, and giving the mixture in warm wine for a period of no more than nine days[10]. It was this kind of magic which relied upon natural ingredients and the power inherent in nature to produce the desired effect, which was later designated 'Natural Magic', as opposed to the 'Demonic Magic' supposedly practised by witches.

But Pliny's second type of remedy clearly depended for its success on the operation of more than natural powers, even if these were not always referred to. 'I find in my sources,' he said, 'that a head cold is brought to an end if one kisses a mule's nostrils'.[11] Anyone suffering from a painful spleen should have a fresh sheep's spleen put over the correct spot, the operator announcing that he or she is doing this in order to effect a cure, after which the sheep's spleen is to be enclosed within the wall of the patient's bedroom, the plaster being sealed thrice nine times with a signet-ring while the intention to cure is repeated.[12] The ring, or a stone set into the ring, may either have had some magical image or characters engraved upon it, or the impression left in the wet plaster may have identified the sufferer, just as it would have done in the wax of a legal document. Prayer in the Greek and Roman worlds signified obligation on both sides. It implied reciprocity – I give in the expectation of receiving from you in return – and thus created or reinforced a kind of pact between deity and worshipper, a situation common to official cultus as well as to private magic. We have already seen Lucan questioning the basis of this pact in relation to magic, and this notion of a pact was to become the key point in later criminal charges levelled against all workers of magic, including witches.

Pliny also gives recipes for amulets: the tail of a python sewn into gazelle skin with deer sinew and bound to the upper left arm is a charm against epilepsy[13]; a caterpillar wrapped in linen cloth which is then tied round three times, with three knots, while the operator announces the purpose of the amulet, wards off quartan fever[14]; and a snake's sloughed skin tied to the loins will ease the pains of childbirth[15]. Closely allied to this type of amulet are those which are intended to counteract malicious magic directed towards oneself or one's family. The most common and most feared example of this malevolence was perhaps the evil eye which was thought to have its roots in envy and personal hatred.

Pliny passed on the reports of Greek writers on the subject. There were non-Greek peoples who could bewitch others merely by looking at them, and even kill if they stared at their victim in anger.[16] Cicero noted that any woman who had a double pupil could inflict harm with her glance[17], and Plutarch observed that children could be particularly susceptible to this kind of magical influence because their physical constitutions were not yet sufficiently developed to be able to withstand it.[18] Counteractive magic might consist of spitting or wearing an appropriate amulet. This often took the form of a *fascinum*, an image in the shape of a penis, which was not only worn by individuals but also attached to the chariot of a general celebrating a military triumph[19], or built into the wall of one's house as a means of permanent protection.

For Pliny, as we have seen, astrology was that branch of magic known as 'divination'. But this was not the only means of divination available to the ancient world; for while astrology looked to the planets for messages concerning the future and the will of deities, almost anything, in fact, could be turned into an instrument for that purpose. Official cultus approved of oracles such as those at Delphi and Cumae where the deity spoke through a resident priestess; augury, which observed the flight of birds; and extispicy, which examined the entrails of sacrificed animals. But 'unofficial' divination made use of all kinds of inanimate objects such as fire, water, mirrors, bones – inscribed or plain – and even sieves, the latter being used by old women to diagnose sickness in sheep (presumably by suspending the sieve in some fashion and seeing which way it turned in response to suggestions or questioning).

'Unofficial' divination also had its oracular priestesses, *engastrimythoi*, 'speakers from the stomach', who became possessed by a non-human spirit which then spoke through them[20], not really different from those at Delphi and other big cult centres, except that the latter had state and public approval while the former, on the whole, did not. Such possession by divinities or spirits brings us back to the question of how and why such entities should consent to occupy a human being and answer questions. The answer, as we have seen, lay in the notion that intercourse between humans and non-humans invariably took the form of a business transaction, and this can be seen in the most common of these evocations, the raising of the dead. The fifth-century BC dramatist, Aeschylus, included in one of his plays an extraordinary scene wherein the Persian Queen, Atossa, pours libations to the dead and invites the male chorus to chant with a view to summoning the ghost of her husband, the late King Darius.[21] Here, the ghost and the divinities of the afterlife are offered wine; but such simple oblations were not always enough and we hear also of human sacrifice, principally of young boys, by necromancers wishing thereby to appease the infernal spirits[22], while the matricide Emperor Nero was said to have tried, with the help of magicians, to raise his mother's ghost in order to persuade her to soften her rage against him[23].

The major aspect of this 'unofficial' magic which was likely to trouble people, no matter to which class of society they belonged, was malefice, harmful magic which might cause difficulties, illness, poverty, or even death to the person against whom it was directed, or to his family, his animals, or his goods. I have already mentioned erotic magic which was intended to render someone impotent, the malevolence of certain *pharmaka/veneficia*, and the accusations of hostile magic which resulted in large numbers of executions during the second decade of the second century BC. Rome's earliest law-code, the *Twelve Tables* (451–450 BC), contained legislation against anyone chanting an evil incantation with the intention of doing someone else harm or enticing away his fruit or corn[24], a charge which was not merely theoretical as we can see from the case of Gaius Furius Chresimus, a freedman, who was accused of just such an offence by envious neighbours who thought the high yields of his farm must be due to *veneficia*, acts of harmful magic[25].

A favourite means of working magical harm, however, consisted of *defixiones*, curse-tablets, made from pieces of lead on which were inscribed the disaster being wished on the victim. These might be used for almost any hostile purpose, to ill-wish a potential political or business-rival, a rival in love or the unresponsive object of one's passion, or to call down the vengeance of deities both official and unofficial. Sometimes, as in erotic magic, the notion of binding might play an important part in the magical conception:

> I bind Iphemythanes and Andosthenes and Simmias and Dromon. I
> bind their hands and feet in the presence of Hermes the restrainer:
> I also bind their soul, their tongues, their work, and their profits
>
> Gager: *Curse Tablets*, no. 67

These tablets might also be accompanied by or incorporated into magical instruments such as voodoo dolls, whose appearance, stuck through with pins, can easily be misunderstood. The pins may not necessarily be there as weapons to cause pain in the equivalent part of the victim's body, but as markers to draw the attention of the gods or goddesses or non-human entities, on whose power the magician is relying for the success of his piece of magic, to those specific parts of the body he wants affected. It is the words of the spell which matter and give the required clues to the kind of magic which is being worked. *Defixiones* are found in all kinds of places. Sometimes they have been buried in secret, often within a grave if the assistance of a ghost was required or the object of the spell had died and was being pursued after death. When someone successfully hexed to death Germanicus Caesar, the Emperor Tiberius's nephew, for example, an investigation of the walls and floor of the room wherein he died turned up pieces of human body, clearly pulled from the funeral pyre, written incantations and curses, *defixiones* with his name scratched on them, and other magical objects intended to send the soul of the living to its destruction.[26] Sometimes, however, these tablets were left in open spaces so that anyone might read them and know who was being attacked and why; an admirable way, all magic apart, to ruin a reputation or create a climate of fear.

There are two general points worth noting about these curse-tablets. Some are very simple and could have been made at home. Others, however, contain long, elaborate formulae along with magical names and figures and it is likely that whoever made these either took professional advice or was himself a professional magician. We should therefore bear in mind the existence of such a professional group, skilled or unskilled, genuine or charlatan as the case may be, and remember that these magicians would not have emerged in the first place or continued to operate without the active participation of a clientele which, potentially, comprised a majority of the population. Plato writes of just such professionals:

> Begging, charlatan priests of foreign divinities, and people who foretell the future, go to the doors of the rich and get them to believe that they have persuaded the gods, by means of sacrifices and incantations, to endow them with power to expiate (with the help of things which give pleasure and [magical] banquets) any intentional wrong committed by an individual or his ancestors; and that if the client wants to harm one of his enemies, it will cost very little to harm him, whether he be

respectable or not, since (they claim) they employ incantations and binding magic to persuade the gods to do as they are told.

Republic 2.364b–c

Plato was both rich and intellectual. People such as he tended to despise professional magicians and, indeed, magic as a whole. This is partly because they were capable of formulating what appeared to be rational arguments against it, but also partly because they associated magic with 'people who are not like us', in other words, non-citizens, women, the poor, foreigners, and slaves; and because so much surviving information about magic in all its aspects is to be found in the writings of men rather like Plato, we must always try to be conscious of its origins and make allowance for the sceptical hostility or social disdain which runs through their works like a thread.

Now, all this magic was self-evidently beyond normal human powers. Magicians could operate only if they had special knowledge of the laws of nature, which permitted them to achieve apparent wonders – the type of magic later known as 'natural' because it manipulated nature according to her own innate laws and did not depend on supernatural or preternatural powers – or if they entered into some kind of pact or alliance with divinities or semi-divine entities, and relied on their more than human, more than natural abilities to produce extraordinary effects. In the Classical world, the majority of these non-human beings were *daimones*, described by Plato as intermediaries between deities and humans, with the power to transmit all forms of prophecy, priestly skills concerning sacrifices, the rites practised at initiation into secret (but officially-approved) cults, and incantations, as well as all types of divination and necromancy.[27] Plutarch added that *daimones* do not possess a pure or unadulterated divine nature, but are susceptible to pleasure and pain and the other experiences attendant upon physical existence, a dilution of their other-worldliness which means that, like human beings, some *daimones* are good and others bad.[28] It does not take much imagination, then, to see in these entities the forerunners of those evil spirits to whose agency was attributed the power of witches and other magical operators during medieval and early modern times.

Politicians and other figures of authority, as we have seen, were troubled by all the occult sciences, not simply by magic. It seemed to them that any appeal to non-human powers unapproved by the state ran the danger of being subversive of good order and necessary tradition. The identity of the state, indeed (and by this one means a relatively small community such as the city-state and its environs, as well as the larger social conglomerates), was intimately bound up with its traditional modes of religious, civic, and social behaviour and anything which did not form an integral part of any of these − the Egyptian cult of Isis or the Syrian cult of Cybele, for example, both of which caused grave suspicion and disdain in Rome − was likely to find itself the target of legal hostility. In Athens, acts of maleficent magic involving *pharmaka* were probably tried as straightforward cases of murder[29]. In Rome, apart from the Twelve Tables I have mentioned already, the principal law concerned with similar forms of magic was passed in 81 BC. Known as the *lex Cornelia de sicariis et veneficiis* (Sulla's Law dealing with Murder and Acts of Poisoning or Maleficent Magic), this ostensibly concentrated on simple poisoning, but was quickly extended to include magical *venena* and the practice of those rituals which usually accompanied the gathering of herbs and their preparation and administration for magical purposes. This we can see from a celebrated trial in *c*.AD 160. Apuleius of Madaura, a Platonist philosopher, had married a wealthy widow and when she died in mysterious circumstances, her relatives charged Apuleius with being a magician and causing the woman's death by administering a love-potion or *venenum*; and the law under which they charged him was the *lex Cornelia*, interpreted to cover these particular circumstances.

What concerned both the Greek and Roman legislation was clearly whether a specific harm had been done to an individual, and in as far as no such harm could be proven, the accused might be acquitted, as indeed was Apuleius. On the other hand, given different circumstances, a less than favourable social standing of the defendant, and a surrounding atmosphere of panic, such as we saw in the *veneficia* cases of 184-183 and 180-179 BC, the result could be fatal for more than a single defendant and large numbers of people might find themselves caught up in a spiral of accusations. The parallel with later intense bursts of witch-prosecution in Europe is not far to seek. It is also worth marking for future reference that, even though magic did not constitute a coherent whole, the authorities were less and less inclined as time went on to distinguish between popular and learned or ritual magic. The more magical operators claimed extensive and extraordinary powers, the more representatives of official orthodoxy allowed themselves to assume that, for all practical purposes, there was little difference between calling upon *daimones* to assist in the preparation of magical philtres, invoking the dead to ascertain the future, and praying to unofficial deities to elevate one's spirit towards communion with the godhead. All became undesirable and, in the eyes of the law, boundaries between native and foreign practices were blurred.

❦

We can see from this very brief outline that although magic was ubiquitous in the Greek and Roman worlds, it did not actually constitute anything like a pseudo- or unofficial religious cult with a coherent theology of its own. There were, in fact, different kinds of magic, co-existent and not necessarily available to everyone. There was ritual magic, for example, learned and bookish and because of those very attributes, exclusive. This was the kind often known as *theurgia*, 'a divine work' which sought to raise the consciousness of the practitioner so that it contacted the highest form of the Divine – 'When the soul has been united with the various parts of everything in turn, and with all the divine powers which pervade them, then the soul is brought to the undivided Creator and is entrusted to his keeping'[30] – an attempt at religious mysticism, in fact, and a far cry form the world of curse-tablets, love-charms, and curative herbal mixtures and incantations. There was what one might call 'official' magic, the auguries and other divinations performed on behalf of the state as part of its public cultus, and, dwarfing both of these in the range and variety of its practices and practitioners, there was 'popular' magic, embracing rituals the operator could work for him or herself, those which required professional advice, and those which could be performed only by professional magicians. The emergence of such a professional group is difficult to trace, but the growth during the Hellenistic period of magic as a craft requiring particular skills and even training suggests that the professional magician, male or female, came to prominence at about this time.

Literature, of course, was not slow to seize upon the magical operator as a figure who could be used for a number of different literary purposes: to express, in physical form, certain aspects of divine or divine-like power, to act as a target for the writer's scepticism (real or claimed), or to impart to the reader or listener the pleasurable *frisson* which comes from insulated presentation of the formidable powers evoked by those bold enough to attempt to harness them to their own will and purpose. One of the earliest portraits of such a practitioner comes from Book 10 of Homer's *Odyssey*. Her name was Circe and she lived on a fabulous island later identified as a promontory in Latium in Italy. Odysseus, battling against the ill will of some of the gods to make his way back home after the fall of Troy, is driven ashore there, and some of his men meet Circe at her house in the middle of a forest. At their arrival, mountain wolves and lions come to greet them, fawning around them like dogs. But the men are struck by fear because, despite the creatures' animal appearance, they are standing on two legs, like men, and indeed Homer tells us that Circe had subdued them ('stroked them into acquiescence' is his colourful phrase) by giving them wicked *pharmaka*. Circe invites the men inside. All save one accept food and a mixture of honey and wine laced with baneful *pharmaka*, which they proceed to drink. Immediately, Circe strikes them with a magic rod and they turn into pigs. Odysseus, however, is saved from a similar fate when he meets her because the god Hermes gives him a piece of counter-magic, a herb with a dark root and a milky-white flower. The amulet works, and at Odysseus's insistence Circe agrees to remove her metamorphic magic from his men, which she does by smearing them with yet another *pharmakon*.[31]

Here, then, we are introduced to two instruments of magic: the herbs and the rod. The latter appears elsewhere in Homer's epics as a means whereby authority is exercised: Athene restores Odysseus to youth, for example, by touching him with such an instrument[32], and Hermes sends soldiers to sleep in a similar fashion[33]. Circe, however, is not a human being. Her father was one of the Titans, a race of gods older than the Olympians, and so she partakes of their divine nature. Homer depicts her as a beautiful, seductive woman, able and consistently eager to ensnare a man and yet unwilling to retain him in human form for, as she explains in a mixture of fear and bewilderment to Odysseus after her magic has failed to work on him, 'no other man, not one, has resisted these *pharmaka*'.

Five hundred years later, during the third century BC, Apollonius of Rhodes penned another portrait of a woman with magical powers. Like Circe, she is not entirely human, being a granddaughter of the Sun, but whereas Circe is more or less portrayed as a goddess, Medea is presented as a woman, desperately enamoured of the hero of the epic, Jason, and willing to abandon her own family and people for love of him, and to kill on his behalf. Like Circe, she possesses magical *pharmaka* ('some which do good, others which are destructive'), but unlike Circe, she wields the power of the evil eye and uses incantations against her enemies[34]; and whereas Circe's hostile magic seems to be directed almost with indifference towards its objects, Medea is a woman of violent emotions which Apollonius describes as 'abominable infatuation', attributing them to Eros, not the god of love so much as the god of sexual passion. Magic, sex, and ruthless wickedness have thus been linked with a woman, thereby providing a combination we shall find in late medieval guides to what a witch is like.

By the time we reach the first century AD, these portraits have taken a more theatrical turn. When Ovid describes Medea, for example, he invests her with the character of a professional magician and provides her with a setting which may owe something to reality, but which gives the impression of a stage set prepared for a leading actress's *tirade*:

When the moon shone at her most full and, with her visible form unbroken, looked upon the lands [of earth], Medea came out of the house clothed in garments which were not girded up with a belt. Her feet were bare, her hair flowed down upon her shoulders, and without any companion, she roamed hither and thither through the deep silences of the middle of the night. A deep sleep had set free from their bonds humans, birds and animals. The hedgerow was silent, no sound at all. Leaves were silent and made no movement. The damp air was silent. Only the stars glittered. To these Medea stretched out her arms. Three times she turned in a circle. Three times she took water from a stream and sprinkled it on her hair flowing loose. Three times she opened her mouth and uttered drawn-out, shrieking yells

Metamorphoses 7.180–91

This is an important passage for understanding later perceptions of a witch, for the normal social conventions are here overthrown and we are presented with their opposites. Everything is set free from the expected ties which govern proper – that is officially-approved – behaviour. Women usually had their dresses tightly bound under the breast with a belt; Medea has removed this restraint. Respectable women wore their hair braided or crimped and ornamented; Medea has left hers free. People and animals act according to social or instinctual imperatives during the day; at night they are liberated from these by sleep. People talk during the day, and their lives are penetrated by a variety of noises; Ovid stresses the silence of night when even nature makes not a single expected sound. Speech is also normally governed by a whole range of rules and conventions; Ovid says that Medea 'sets her mouth free' when she gives vent to her ululations. When people speak, they usually try to be coherent and comprehensible; Medea's howls make no such sense, but express only raw excitement as she works herself up into the emotional state appropriate to invocation of the powers of the underworld. Even Medea's footsteps do not conform to normative behaviour, for when she leaves the house, instead of moving purposefully from one point to another, she wanders about aimlessly, constantly changing direction.

This is a world constituted according to the principles of inversion whereby order becomes disorder and the positive qualities of everyday, accepted, officially-approved living are turned into their negative counterparts, much as happened later in medieval carnivals. Even daylight must be subverted, and Medea conducts her invocation by full moon at the hour of midnight. As Lucan expressed it in his description of the powers of Thessalian women, long famous for their command of the magical arts, 'the orderly process of change in nature comes to a halt; the hours of daylight are extended and cling to a drawn-out night; the upper air does not obey nature's law; and when it hears the Thessalians' incantation, the universe which usually rushes headlong turns lethargic and comes to a halt'.[35]

Now, these verses are a preliminary to Lucan's lengthy portrait of a 'witch', Erictho, whose theatricality almost puts that of Ovid's Medea in the shade. Whatever baneful magic the Thessalian women could work, he says, is not wicked enough for Erictho 'who had turned her degraded skill in the direction of novel rituals'[36], and his word 'degraded' implies that her magic was the opposite of that of which official religion might approve since it involved both moral impurity and physical filthiness. We can see what he means by this at once. Apparently, Erictho is a necromancer who has chosen to live in a graveyard and rifles not only long-established tombs, but even fresh funeral pyres and the crosses on which criminals have died in order to gather therefrom pieces of flesh and bone and nail for use in her rites. The Romans were accustomed to bury their dead beyond the city-limits, and thus in as much as Erictho has chosen to live in a cemetery, she has voluntarily placed herself outwith normal, approved society. She is, in fact, in every sense beyond the pale, and her house which is properly the house of a dead person, her intercourse with the dead rather than with the living, and her deliberate reversal of waking hours, which makes her active at night rather than during the day, are clear signs that she is inhabiting that world of inversion which was rapidly being perceived as appropriate to *all* workers of magic.

Unlike Circe or Medea, however, both of whom are portrayed as at least relatively young and beautiful, Erictho is said to be old and hideously ugly. The very touch of her feet scorches the seeds of a cornfield which is usually fertile, and her breath ruins any breezes which do not carry plague along with them. So Lucan has added three more important features to the tradition: witches desecrate graves to supply themselves with magical material; they are old, ugly women; and the purpose of their magic and their lives is essentially destructive. Nor is this all. Erictho, we are told, 'slits open the womb in a way not called for by nature, and drags forth the unborn child to place it upon the flames of an altar'.[37] The murder of babies or children thus becomes part of the composite picture of a witch, as we can see further, for example, in Horace's *Epode* 5 which describes four 'witches' preparing to murder a young lad by burying him in earth up to his neck and then letting him starve to death, with a view to using parts of his body later to make a love-philtre.

We have seen that there was often official disquiet about the very notion of the efficacy of magic, and disdain for the practitioners thereof. One way of expressing that disquiet was to bring the operators to court and execute the guilty. Another was to pour scorn on magic, representing it either as deliberate cozenage or as ridiculous fantasizing. Cicero dismissed 'the extravagant inventions of magicians and Egyptians' together with 'the beliefs of the common people, which are turned into total inconsistency by their ignorance of the truth' as constituting a kind of insanity[38], and lamented that 'superstition, which has spread throughout the nations, has overpowered almost everyone's mind and has seized hold of humanity's moral and intellectual weakness'[39]. But it was perhaps Pliny the Elder who expressed most forcefully the dislike felt for magic and its operators by an educated, career-conscious Roman:

> In the previous part of my work, I have had frequent occasion to expose the emptiness and silliness of magic...and I shall continue to lay these bare. There are few subjects which deserve to be spoken of at greater length, if only because this most dishonest of skills has dominated the whole world age after age after age. [Then Pliny explains that magic arose from medicine, and thereafter aligned itself with religion and astrology to complete its hold on people's imagination.] Thus, having gripped people's emotions and understanding in its threefold shackle, it grew to such an eminence that even these days it has the upper hand over the greater part of the world's nations, and in the East commands those who are kings over other kings.
>
> *Naturalis Historia* 30.1

The dislike of the learned, then, was tinged a little with fear. But this fear could be mitigated by lacing criticism with contempt. Thus, Propertius describes an old brothel-keeper, whom he imagines on her death-bed, coughing up phlegm and blood between her decayed teeth. She used to be very skilled in magic, he says, 'daring enough to impose her commands on the moon she had enchanted, and to disguise her human form under that of the nocturnal wolf. With her finger-nail, she ripped out the eyes of innocent ravens so that, by her craft, she could blind husbands on the watch. She consulted vampire-owls/'witches' on the best way to draw my blood, and gathered mucous secretion from a pregnant mare to use against me'.[40] Clearly, Propertius is nervous of her, even though she is dead; but he spices his description with frequent comments on how old the woman was, how filthy and ragged her clothes were, how tattered the sheets on her death-bed. He even draws attention to her stinking breath, and to the fact that at the end of her life she had little hair left.

Horace, on the other hand, preferred to mock. *Satires* 1.8 is put into the mouth of a wooden statue of the god Priapus who remembers when he was set up in a graveyard and, on one occasion, watched two old, ugly necromancers, Canidia and Sagana, sacrificing a black lamb to summon up ghosts whom they could then question about the future. The two women also had with them voodoo dolls, one made of wool, the other of wax, but as they were busying themselves with the closing acts of their ritual, Priapus farted and the two women ran away, Horace commenting sardonically, 'to the sound of loud laughter and derision you might see Canidia lose her teeth and Sagana her lofty wig, with herbs and spells falling from their arms'.

It is impossible in so short a compass to do justice to the immense range and subtlety of Classical magic and to the changing reactions to it over the centuries between Homer and the establishment of Christianity as the preferred Imperial religion. My aim has been, rather, to highlight some of those aspects of both which turned out to be significant in the development of the late medieval and early modern concept of 'witch' and 'witchcraft'. The intentions of the magical operations are not peculiar to Greece and Rome or to any other historical period, of course. The desire to manipulate love, cure intractable diseases, uncover the future, and harm those one perceives as enemies is universal. Nor is the disapproval and suspicion of authority, religious or secular, confined to the Graeco-Roman tradition. But that tradition did pass down from Classical to later times certain concepts of magical operators peculiar to itself, and these concepts are embodied in the terminology relating to magic and magical practitioners, thus providing perhaps the most important links between the various stages of that tradition.

Let us take, for example, the reference to vampire-owls in the passage of Propertius quoted above. Propertius's word for these is *striges* (singular *strix*), and it became one of the standard words for 'witch' in the later period. Essentially 'screech-owl', it carried a good deal of folkloric baggage in addition to its ornithological reference. Ovid gives a good summary:

> They have a very large head, goggle eyes, and beaks which are good for tearing. Their wings are grey, the colour of old people's hair, and their nails each end in a hook. They fly at night, seeking out young children who have no nurse, seize them bodily from their cradles, and molest them. It is said that with their beaks they rip off pieces from the intestines of unweaned babies and that their throats are full of the blood they have drunk. They are called *striges* because it is their habit to screech at night in such a way that it raises the hair on the back of your neck. They may have been born as birds, or they may have become birds through enchantment, old women whose shape has been changed into that of a bird by a Marsian incantation.
>
> *Fasti* 6.133-42

The *strix*, therefore, could be understood as an old woman who was able to change her shape by magic, who moved about at night, and deliberately hunted babies and small children, eating their flesh and drinking their blood. It is a folk tradition Ovid mentions elsewhere, describing an aged brothel-keeper who was skilled in magic. 'I have an idea,' he says, 'that she changes her shape, covering her old woman's body with feathers, and flits about through the shadows of the night'[41]; and the concept is repeated in another word which later became a standard term for 'witch' – *lamia*, a bogey-figure from mythology who, like the *strix*, used to devour people, especially children.

Another term which became equally common was *saga*. Cicero tells us that it is connected with a verb 'to have a distinct feeling about something' – compare English 'presentiment' or 'foreboding' – and links the word with old women.[42] She is thus, at basis, a diviner, like the *sortilega* (again later 'witch') who casts lots and interprets the future from their markings or from the patterns they form once they have fallen, although the psychic powers of the *saga*, who was dependent on personal feeling, were obviously thought of as operating independently of aids such as dice or other inscribed material. The *saga* in practice, however, did more than just predict future events. She could release someone from another's enchantment[43], manufacture a magical wax image and so curse the person it represented[44], or avert an unwanted future event which her client had seen in a dream[45]. The *saga* was also said to be capable of maleficent magic such as changing those with whom she was offended into animals, or preventing a woman from giving birth at the proper time. She might also use her magical powers to escape being lynched by a mob of her fellow townspeople.[46]

So four of the most common Latin words for a female practitioner of magic imply murderous hostility towards babies and children, or an ability to interpret the future. In literary usage these were supplemented by two others which also carried on into medieval and early modern times: (a) *venefica*, a maker of poison/herbal concoction with magical accompaniments/baneful magic; and (b) *Thessalia*, a woman from Thessaly which was a region of Greece notorious in ancient times for the extraordinary command over nature supposedly held by some of its women, and hence any woman to whom such powers were attributed. Already, therefore, a tradition can be discerned in the very language which was used and would continue to be used by both religious and secular authority, which suggested that female operators of magic were potentially very dangerous (at the very least, undesirable), along with the implication that their activities should be regarded as probably criminal.

Now, all six words appear over and over again in later records, along with others less frequently employed, and since they imply the possession of different powers, some beneficent, some malefi-cent, the habit of using the single English word 'witch' to translate them will certainly disguise this variety and may well mislead the reader. It has been suggested that by the later period differentia-tion between the words had more or less been lost, and certainly the Classical use of *saga*, which we have just seen, may seem to lend support to this notion. But had people not preserved at least some notional distinction in their kinds between these terms, one would have expected most of them to disappear over the centuries, leaving just one word, as in English 'witch', to cover the basic concept. The fact that this did not happen suggests that later writers were still aware of the differences and, if they were careful at all, used the different words to emphasize what one may call the distinguishing or principal magical skill of the individual under discussion. To call someone *saga* or *strix*, then, gave the reader a signal: 'this is what I want you to think of at this particular moment; these are the emotional reactions I want to elicit from you'. The term did not, and was not meant to act as a strait-jacket, just as 'teacher' may indicate someone who specializes in teaching one subject but can be called upon, according to circumstances, to teach more than one: or 'doctor', someone who may specialize in one area of medicine, but who may still be asked from time to time to exercise skill in another. 'Witch', therefore, is a highly limiting term for *strix, lamia, saga, sortilega, venefica*, etc. and anyone who reads witchcraft literature needs to be aware that the translation 'witch' may be referring to a remarkable variety of types of magical practitioner.

Different kinds of magic: different kinds of magical operator. These were well understood by everyone in the Graeco-Roman period, and this understanding was transmitted to the future which transposed and modified details according to the geographical area in which the Classical tradition arrived. But the biggest shift, at least in official perception, happened when Christianity became the approved religion of the state. For Christian theology introduced people to a particular view of Satan, and his evolving role in the eternal scheme of things was going to make a major difference to the way magic and magical operators were viewed by authority.

II

—❧ CHAPTER TWO ❧—

Enter the Christian Witch

Not long after Christianity began to make an impact on the Roman world, it became clear that the new religion had two major struggles on its hands. First, there were the deviations from orthodox theology, the heresies which rose and fell during the early Christian centuries, concerning themselves at this time principally with the exact nature of Jesus and his relation to God the Father. Secondly came the problem of magic. Since magical practitioners were ubiquitous, and since their stock in trade consisted of claims to exercise powers beyond the merely natural or human, the moment non-Christians realized that Jesus was credited with miraculous cures and exorcisms, and that the burgeoning Church was offering its converts rituals such as baptism and the eucharist – which purported to drive away evil spirits and change the substance of bread and wine into the body and blood of the new god – they maintained that Jesus himself was a magician, a wonder-worker of a type familiar to the ancient world, and that what his Church called 'sacraments' were actually no different from rites of magic.

This posed a problem. On the one hand, it allowed Christian missionaries access to the pagan willingness to accept, more or less without reservation, the possibility of the miraculous, and hence belief in Christ's resurrection and the efficacious reality of the sacraments; on the other, it required Christian apologists to explain why their miracles (whether those of Christ himself or of the Apostles or of later saints), were genuine, while those of pagan magicians such as Simon Magus or Apollonius of Tyana were fraudulent. Crucial to this argument were the figures of Satan and the *daimones*, and the eventual formulation of Christian teaching on these figures became the key element in later explanations of how witches were able to operate and why God allowed them to do so.

The *daimones* of Classical literature, as we have seen, were semi-divine entities who acted as intermediaries between human beings and gods and goddesses, and it was they who enabled workers of magic to achieve their effects and wonders. Saint Peter warned pagans that if they refused to listen to the Christian message, they would be possessed by *daimones* (here clearly evil spirits) who would thereafter control them for their own wicked purposes[1], and in the eyes of Saint Augustine of Hippo, the *daimones* were equally dangerous, being frauds who seek to play tricks on humans whom they actually control[2]. Any kind of magic, he said, depends on a pact between the magical operator and the *daimon*, and he listed by way of example all types of magical objects people tie round their necks or arms or waists, and any remedies for illness not approved by regular doctors, whether these were in the form of incantations, written magical characters, amulets, or symbolic dancing.[3] The Greek Church Father, Origen, went a stage further and said that 'magicians consort with evil spirits and invoke them in accordance with what they have learned and what they wish to do'.[4] The verb here translated as 'consort with' is capable of more than one meaning. It indicates keeping company with, being familiar with, but it may also imply having sexual intercourse with, and here we find a hint of that later charge which was brought against witches – that they copulated with Satan or his evil spirits either during the Sabbat or on other occasions when they met him individually.

I mentioned Simon Magus and Apollonius of Tyana. Both men were, among other things, wonder-working magicians who were considered to represent a threat, however minimal, to the leaders of the Christian community. Simon appears in the New Testament *Acts* and in the apocryphal *Acts of Peter*. Already possessing some reputation as a magician, he got himself baptized and asked the Apostles to sell him their gift of healing – hence the term 'simony' – a request they spurned with anger, but then, in a wonder-working competition with Saint Peter in the presence of the Emperor Nero, he managed to use his magical powers to make himself fly through the air until he was brought down to earth with a crash by the superior power of the saint, and thus lost the contest. Apollonius was accorded an even greater reputation, and his life, as recounted by the second to third century AD Greek philosopher Philostratus, contains a number of incidents which may be parallelled with some in the life of Jesus. His miraculous birth was announced beforehand to his mother by a *daimon*. He cured the sick, exorcized demoniacs, was able to predict future events, was twice arrested by the Roman authorities and made to stand trial before the Emperor (first Nero, then Domitian), appeared miraculously in a cave to two of his followers who thought he was a ghost, and upon his death was assumed into the heavens but continued to appear to and teach his followers.

Both these lives demonstrate that people of the early Christian centuries expected religious or philosophical leaders to be able to perform wonders even if, like Jesus and Apollonius, they sometimes refused to do so. Christianity, therefore, did not have a choice over abolishing or ignoring magic. Magic had to be accommodated, and where it could not be condemned *tout court*, its more potent or irretractable manifestations had to be re-interpreted in the light of developing Christian theology. Hence the need to deal with *daimones*.

In a work attributed to the theologian Dionysius the Areopagite the hierarchy of Heaven was set out in some detail. Seraphim, Cherubim, and Thrones constituted the first rank of angels; then came Dominions, Powers, and Authorities; and finally Principalities, Archangels and Angels[5], artistic representation of whom as winged figures in human shape – only one of their possible forms, to be sure, but the one which particularly touched the public imagination – had its origins in Classical times. But if Heaven had its hierarchy, so did Hell. Various Church Fathers, relying first on the *Apocalypse* and then on the apocryphal *Book of Enoch*, explained that there had been a rebellion in Heaven, with extraordinary consequences:

> Now war arose in heaven, Michael and his angels fighting against the dragon; and the dragon and his angels fought, but they were defeated and there was no longer any place for them in heaven. And the great dragon was thrown down, that ancient serpent, who is called the Devil and Satan, the deceiver of the whole world – he was thrown down to the earth; and his angels were thrown down with him.
>
> Revelation 12.7-9

'Some of these,' added Athenagoras, 'fell in love with women and fathered giants upon them; and thereafter the souls of these giants became evil spirits which wander through the world and seduce human beings into errors, and into the greatest sins of idolatry and lust'.[6] 'Lustful angels,' went on the *Clementine Recognitions*, 'teach that, by means of certain magical invocations, evil spirits can be made to obey human beings'[7], and we can see in Coptic magical texts, for example, details of this story of the fall of Satan and his angels incorporated into rituals to be performed for various purposes.

The names of some of the most important of these angels were known, of course, as it was essential for the purposes of invocations to call up precisely the spirit one intended: Azazel, Belial, Beelzebub, Asmodeus, Ashtaroth, and Lilith, the female demon who was turned by later legend into Satan's mother and thus became a grotesque parody of the Virgin Mary; and by the fifteenth century we are able to find that evil spirits could also be grouped into categories similar to those of the heavenly angels. Thus, Alfonso de Spina, bishop of Orense, recorded some of their popular names and types:

Just as good angels and blessed souls are divided into nine ranks, so evil spirits fell from these nine into another nine categories, and damned souls along with them. Those evil spirits who belonged to the higher grades of the [heavenly] hierarchy became correspondingly worse and more inferior in that part of the meridian whose ruler the Psalmist has called 'the destruction that wastes at noonday'. But there are popular names for many of these spirits and their various grades. Some are called *fates*, others (in Spanish) *duende*, others *incubi* and *succubi*. Some of them cause wars; others eat and drink with human beings and appear in their dreams. Some are said to be generated from the smell given off by a man and a woman during sexual intercourse, or from planetary rays. Some are hermaphrodites; some are clean and others filthy. Some deceive men and women who are called *jorguinas* or *brujas* in Spanish. Many people claim to have seen spirits of this type and stick to the truth of their assertion.

Fortalitium fidei Book 5, proposition 10

Material creation itself was similarly arranged. At the lowest point in the centre lay earth, formed of the four elements whose imperfection and mutability extended upwards as far as the moon. Beyond this point revolved the seven planets – Moon, Mercury, Venus, Sun, Mars, Jupiter, Saturn – each contained in the wall of its own crystalline sphere, and beyond these the imaginary zone or belt of the zodiac. To the seven planetary spheres were added the crystalline sphere of the sky and the Primum Mobile, the very first part of creation set in motion by God, and whose movement regulated the movements of all the lower spheres. Each planet had its own spirit or angel who could be invoked magically and each planet affected everything below it, including, of course, the elemental world and humanity, by means of invisible rays which might be beneficial or malevolent in their effect according to their particular source and its changing relationship with the other heavenly bodies.

The significance of all this for witches is plain. From being spirit-intermediaries, the *daimones* developed into evil spirits mirroring in their organization and graded powers the angelic hierarchy, and by their fall through the increasingly inferior stages into which the material world was divided, they arrived in the sublunary, elemental region where they degenerated and suffered (though to a lesser degree because of their origins), the same imperfections (though not limitations), as humankind. They became associated with the practice of magic, any magic, and so tainted the conception of magic that it became difficult, if not impossible, for Christian theology to dissociate the practice of magic from traffic with evil spirits. But when it comes to *jorguinas* and *brujas* (different words for 'witch'), De Spina uses a verb capable of more than one meaning. The spirits, he says, 'deceive' them in the sense of 'playing with' them or 'making fools of' them, as well as 'using them for sexual pleasure'. It is thus a complex description of a sinister relationship. The notion of a pact between human beings and *daimones* became deep-seated, and in consequence any act of magic was liable to be interpreted as the effect of a diabolical alliance between evil spirit and human operator. Moreover, the habit grew of blaming evil spirits for any kind of misfortune. God might be all-powerful and all-merciful, but he was perfectly prepared to permit Satan and his evil spirits to punish people's sins, or to test their faith, as the Biblical case of Job famously demonstrated. Angels and evil spirits in their serried ranks turned into opposing armies in a continual war between good and evil and therefore it could be argued that any human being who practised magic was liable to be doing so with the connivance and help of Satan and thus to have aligned him or herself on the side of evil, which meant that he or she must be an enemy of God. The situation was summed up by the fifteenth-century theologian, Pedro Ciruelo:

Anyone who maintains a pact or treaty of friendship with the Devil commits a very grave sin because he is breaking the first commandment and is sinning against God, committing the crime of treason or *lèse majesté*. His action is also contrary to the religious vow he made when he was baptized. He becomes an apostate from Christ, and an idolater who renders service to the enemy of God, the Devil.

Reprobación de las supersticiones y hechizerias, part 1, ch. 2

It should not comes as a surprise, then, to find that one of the most common reactions to someone's possession by an evil spirit was to have the demon 'exorcized', a word based on the Greek 'to set free from an oath'. In the pagan Graeco-Roman world this process was officially regarded with grave suspicion. The jurist Ulpian, for example, refused to take exorcists seriously.

Someone will perhaps acknowledge as doctors those who promise a cure for some part of the body or for a particular physical pain — an ear specialist, let us say, or a specialist in fistulas or the teeth. But one must not acknowledge such a person as a doctor if he has used incantations, if he has uttered [magical] curses, or if (and here I use the common expression employed by charlatans) he has 'exorcized' his patient.

Digest 50.13.1.3

The second-century AD littérateur, Lucian, was even more scathing: 'The exorcist with his halitosis cast out many a *daimon* when he spoke, not because he bound them with an oath, but by the power of his dung-like breath'.[8] Part of the problem, at least, lay in the difficulty some people may have had in distinguishing exorcism from just another magical operation. A prayer attributed to Saint Jerome records one of the formulae to be used by exorcists, a mixture of 'barbaric' names or exclamations, and Greek, Hebrew, and Latin epithets and phrases designating the Trinity, all interspersed with signs of the cross, a format which bears close similarities with a straightforward magical exhortation to spirits:

Hel + Heloym + Heloa + Eheye + Tetragrammaton + Adonay +
Saday + Sabaoth Soter + Emanuel + Alpha + and Omega + First
and Last + of the princes + the end + Holy + Strong + the God +
Immortal + Agla + Jehova + Homousion + Ya + Messiah +
Esereheye + Christ conquers + Christ reigns + Christ commands +
Uncreated Father + Uncreated Son + Uncreated Holy Spirit + By
the sign of the cross free us, o God, from our enemies.

Exorcisms quickly established themselves as battle grounds for
magicians and Christian priests to demonstrate their superior
command over non-human entities – the hagiographies of early
Christian saints are full of these and similar stories – and indeed
so useful was the rite as an exhibition of power that it continued
well past the Reformation as Catholics and Protestants sought
to prove the authenticity of their respective claims to religious
rectitude by publicly expelling evil spirits from demoniacs
considered to be otherwise intractable cases. Illness, accident,
misfortune of all kinds to oneself or one's livestock, adverse
weather, storms at sea, unexpected death – all could be, and
were, attributed to the malice of evil spirits and of their human
assistants: magicians, cunning folk, witches.

But it was not simply *daimones* who were re-interpreted in the
light of Christian theology. Curative magic, too, underwent a
certain degree of transformation. Amulets, for example, were
Christianized by being associated with saints and places of
pilgrimage. The sick made a journey to the shrine of a saint
known to cure illness in general or the pilgrim's disease in
particular, and in the event of a cure or noticeable amelioration
left behind images of eyes, hands, feet and so forth as votive gifts.
In return, they might take away with them tokens depicting the
saint or the shrine as apotropaic amulets to ward off recurrence

of the problem. These tokens could be medallions or rings or arm-bands or pendants; or they could take the form of lockets or ampullae which would contain dust, let us say, from the saint's tomb, or medical pills or potions whose potency would be enhanced by contact with an image of the saint or some other image symbolic of his or her miraculous power. Moreover, it was not an absolute requirement that the sick man or woman perform the pilgrimage in person. If the illness were too severe or economic circumstances too straitened to permit the journey, these tokens were considered capable of passing on some of the saint's curative power to work upon the patient who wore the saintly image or took the medicine fortified by transferred magic.

But nor was it necessary for such amulets to be connected directly with a wonder-working saint. Since illness might well be attributed to the malevolence of a *daimon*, any amulet properly inscribed and empowered would be sufficient. A late antique doctor's stamp, for example, shows the Greek word for 'health' around its face, with the initial of the Greek word for 'death' at its centre, enclosed within the most potent magical sign of the pentagram.

So what was the difference between a cure worked by pagan magic and one worked by Christian miracle? Saint Augustine suggested an answer:

> When magicians do the same kind of things as, on occasion, saints do, their deeds may appear similar, to the naked eye, but they have a quite different intention and a quite different sanction. The former do what they do with a view to their own self-esteem, the latter with a view to the glory of God. The former do what they do as a result of certain concessions they have made (in accordance with their

usual procedure), to the powers which control them – private bargains, for example, or personal acts of poisonous magic [*veneficia*]; whereas the latter operate in public, at the command of him to whom all created things are subject.

De diversis quaestionibus 79.4

Even the trait of envy needed a degree of re-interpretation. This root of the concept of the evil eye (Latin, *fascinatio*) had been an integral part of Mediterranean and Middle Eastern culture from very early times, but now Christianity linked it with the Devil and turned it into one of his chief weapons against humanity. 'When evil spirits (who hate what is beautiful), find people who make moral choices which are entirely favourable to them,' wrote Saint Basil, 'they make full use of those decisions for their own private purpose and employ the eyes of the malicious to work their private intention. Doesn't your skin crawl with horror at the thought of making yourself a servant of a deadly evil spirit?'[9] Envy, of course, unlike, say, ceremonial magic, depends on a social context for its effect. One is not envious of a stranger's crops or livestock or thriving family or general good fortune, but of those belonging to one's neighbour, and thus the evil eye is at its most potent among people who live cheek by jowl. It works, as Plutarch pointed out in the second century AD (depending on a theory as old as Democritus), because emotions stimulate our sense-organs which then pour out streams of particles, the most active and effective of which pass through the eye to infect the air between the originator of the particles and their receiver[10]; and because it behaves as though it were some kind of disease, the evil eye can be counteracted, as in the case of an illness, by apotropaic amulets, Christian images woven into one's clothing, and similar forms of magic.

It is not difficult to see how these beliefs would affect people, especially women, accused in a later period of various crimes making up the general offence known as 'witchcraft'. Women's bodies, it was said, were both potentially and actually noxious, as evidenced by menstruation, and 'when any soul has been excited in an immoderate degree to malice, as happens especially in old women, her gaze is made poisonous and harmful in the way I have described earlier, particularly to children who have bodies which are not strong enough to resist it and easily take a mark impressed upon them. It is also possible that, with God's permission, or because of some secret arrangement, the malignancy of evil spirits (with whom elderly witches [*sortilegae*] have some kind of pact) cooperates with such women for this purpose'.[11] Menstruating women, then, can and do work harm simply because of their physical condition, but after they reach an age when the menses cease, their increased emotional bitterness bursts out in the ability to cast an evil eye. This argument provides an explanation for the association of old or elderly women with a certain type of magic (inevitably bound up with suspicion of a demonic pact), but does not entitle one to draw the conclusion that all 'witches' were old women. Trial records alone contradict this notion which has, unfortunately, found its way into many modern accounts of witchcraft.

In the early Christian centuries, therefore, magic was both accommodated and to some extent re-interpreted in the light of the new religion's developing theology. *Daimones* became evil spirits and in that reincarnation were liable to be associated with every branch of magic because of the supposed pact between them and human beings. Perception of creation itself underwent a change as everything took on a Manichaean aspect: God was mirrored by Satan (even though Satan was always acknowledged at least in theory to be weaker and not divine); angels were divided into ranks and had their counterparts in Hell; creation became a battleground between good and evil, with humanity allowed, by free will, to choose which side it would fight upon. In a world where the practice of magic was ubiquitous, Christians were expected by those they wished to convert to work magic more effectively than their pagan equivalents, and this remained a requirement as long as there were sizeable areas of Europe to be converted – that is, until at least the twelfth century. Saints played a major role in this type of activity. They worked wonders, they cured the sick, they expelled evil spirits, and when death took them, their relics continued the good work. Hence, amulets of all kinds, recast in Christian guise, pursued the magical or miraculous ends once sought purely by pagan magic. Even innate sources of malicious preternatural power such as the evil eye continued to operate, although now they would be countered by rites and symbols made Christian, while those who inflicted the effects of the evil eye upon their neighbours were likely to be seen as adherents of Satan, and therefore idolaters and apostates from the Christian faith.

⚬══✦══⚬

The reaction of the state to this situation was to treat magicians of any kind and their clients as potential trouble-makers or even potential enemies. The collection of edicts known as the *Theodosian Code*, which contained legal *pronunciamenti* from more or less the whole of the fourth century AD, forbade consultation of magicians or diviners, regarded necromancy as dangerous in the highest degree, and imposed the death penalty on practitioners of magic. Those who confessed to working harmful or poisonous magic (*maleficium* and *veneficium*), or had been found guilty thereof by due process of law, were not allowed to appeal against their sentence and their families were liable to lose any possible inheritance: nor were such convicted defendants able to benefit from any of the Imperial pardons issued in honour of Easter or to celebrate a birth in the Imperial family. Indeed, being a worker of harmful magic was considered sufficient cause for a woman to sue her husband for divorce, as though he were a murderer or a violater of graves, and some of the edicts go as far as to describe magic in medical terms, as a pollution which contaminates those who come into contact with it.[12]

Many of these edicts relating to magic date from the mid-fourth century when a series of Emperors felt threatened by external forces, and two in particular, Valens and Valentinian I, were vehemently pro-Christian in strong reaction against the attempt of their predecessor, Julian (360-363), to re-establish the old Roman religion as the state cult. Some of this official unease was understandable. A contemporary historian, Ammianus Marcellinus, for example, describes an elaborate magico-astrological ceremony of 371-372, whose object was to predict the succession to the Imperial throne.[13] But in fact much of the activity which fell under imperial displeasure involved only those varieties of magical practice which had been common for centuries.

If anyone wore round his or her neck amulets against quartan fever or some other illness, or was alleged by malicious testimony to have walked past a grave during the evening (the suggestion being that he or she was a worker of poisonous magic, collecting dreadful things from the graves and the useless playthings of souls which wander in that place), he or she was pronounced guilty and executed.

9.12.14

Such actions were treated, as Ammianus overtly says, as though they amounted to high treason, so clearly the prevailing atmosphere was intensely hostile to the simplest forms of magic, and we learn from Ammianus of other executions, too: of a charioteer who entrusted his pre-pubertal son to a worker of poisonous magic so that he might be instructed in certain secrets forbidden by law[14]; of a man who used love-magic in an attempt to persuade a woman to become his wife[15]; and of a simple-minded old woman who used to cure intermittent fevers by means of a harmless incantation[16]. We even hear of an unfortunate youth in the public baths, who touched first the marble fabric and then his chest with each of his fingers in turn, while reciting the seven vowels of the Greek alphabet, in the hope that this charm would cure his stomach trouble. In the event, however, he was arrested, tortured, and beheaded.[17]

This severity continued. In the sixth century we find the restatement of an earlier law that 'workers of harmful magic, enchanters, senders of storms, and those who throw people's minds into confusion by invoking evil spirits, are to be punished with the full range of available penalties. Those who sacrifice to evil spirits or invoke them with incantations are to be executed. Likewise, anyone who invokes evil spirits, or believes in diviners known as "prophets" or "interpreters of bird-flight" is to be executed'.[18] The *Edict of Theoderic* issued a similar condemnation, but distinguished between 'respectable' offenders, who were to be sent into exile, and offenders from 'the lower classes', who were to be put to death.[19]

In the first half of the seventh century, the *Edicta Langobardorum* took matters a stage further. Anyone who had a free girl or a free woman in his protection and called her a witch (*striga*) lost that right over her, unless he happened to be her father or her brother, and she was then able to place herself and her property under the protection of her relatives or the King; and if anyone lost his temper and called a free girl or a free woman under the protection of someone else a 'prostitute' or a 'witch', he was deprived of the sacrament. Nor was anyone permitted to kill a female servant 'as though she were a witch'.[20] In the first two cases, the word for witch is glossed by the popular term *masca*, literally 'a masked woman', an interesting record of a common belief which turns up frequently in later witchcraft evidence that people were accustomed to attend the witches' Sabbat with their faces covered in some fashion, either by a mask or a cloth.

A century later, the *Capitula de partibus Saxoniae* brought the Devil into it:

> If anyone (deceived by the Devil) believes, as non-Christians do, that some man or woman is a witch (*striga*) and eats people, and on that account burns her or gives her flesh to be eaten by others or eats her himself, he shall be executed.

Likewise:

> If someone makes a human sacrifice to the Devil and, as non-Christians do, makes an offering of him or her to evil spirits, he shall be executed.
>
> *Capitula de partibus Saxoniae*, nos. 6 and 9

Cannibalism, then, was not confined to witches, or so it seems, and sacrifices to *daimones* of one kind or another had long survived the arrival of Christianity as the religion of the Imperial state. But then, a list of non-Christian practices, drawn up in the middle of this same eighth century, reminds us of the context in which both secular and ecclesiastical authorities felt obliged to issue their edicts and denunciations. The list includes sacrilege at the graves of the dead; pagan sacrifices and sacrifices offered to Christian saints; the use of amulets, magical knots, and incantations; consultation of diviners, prophesiers, and magical operators; the construction of images from dough or rags for magical purposes; and the belief that women can eat the moon in a magical act designed to direct men's hearts and emotions.[21]

The state, being the state, consistently attached the death penalty to such practices as these. The Church, however, did not. Its condemnations were just as consistent and just as vehement, but it felt unable, whatever the provocation, to inflict the ultimate penalty, reserving for magical offences those punishments which, in the light of its moral authority, it deemed appropriate. From a plethora of Church Councils between the fourth and eighth centuries, then, we can derive a fairly detailed picture of the range of magical activities which drew down the Church's wrath. Women were forbidden to keep watch in cemeteries[22], presumably for fear they might rifle the graves or invoke the ghosts of the dead; people were not to call angels by names not to be found in Scripture[23] – a prohibition clearly aimed at the long-standing habit of including Hebrew and Egyptian names in invocations; while excessive devotion to certain legitimate angels such as Michael was also forbidden[24], presumably on the grounds that it might be mistaken for something akin to pagan worship. Using the Bible for divination was condemned[25], as indeed was any other sort of divination[26]. Pope Zacharias made this clear in a letter to Saint Boniface (1 April 743):

In regard to the New Year celebrations, divinations, amulets, incantations, and other practices which you say are observed in accordance with non-Christian practice at the Church of Saint Peter the Apostle, or in the city of Rome, We consider these to be wrong and to be pernicious for Us and for every Christian...and because they were beginning to raise their heads again, We abolished them all from the day when the grace of God commanded Us, unworthy as We are, to act in the Apostle's place.

If such things could be seen in the very capital of Christian Europe, it is not surprising that four years later Saint Boniface felt obliged to inform Cuthbert, the Archbishop of Canterbury, that he had issued instructions that every bishop was to make a tour of his diocese once a year and root out all remnants of pagan worship, including sacrifices to the dead, divination, the wearing of amulets, and the use of incantations. Such visitations, however, seem to have had little or no lasting effect, for in the second half of the ninth century, we find Archbishop Hincmar of Rheims recording:

The story of the sacrileges I have uncovered takes a long time to recount – bones belonging to human corpses, the quenched ashes and cinders [from funeral pyres], hairs and tufts from the genitalia of men and women, threads of many different colours, herbs of various kinds, small shells, little bits of snake, all enchanted by incantations. But after people have been set free from these, and cured by the blessing of the Church, they have been able once more to perform their marital duty and pleasure. There are those, too, who were in the habit of clothing or veiling themselves in enchanted garments. Practitioners of magic [*sortiarii*] have sent some people mad by giving them something to drink, and others by giving them something to eat. Witches [*strigae*] have bewitched some men with their incantations and rendered them impotent. Witches [*lamiae*], or should I say 'prostitutes', have taken away some men's strength, and apparently evil spirits known as 'Dusii' have taken the form of men for whom certain women were burning with desire, and thus had sexual intercourse with them. But these people, male and female, who were once smothered and degraded by diabolical apparitions, have been restored to health by the power of God, and the exorcisms and antidotes of the Church.

De divortio Lotharii et Tetbergae = *PL* 125.717-18

Penitentials, written for the guidance of parish priests, provide another source of information about the interweaving of pre-Christian and Christian beliefs and practices in communities which were already converted, if only in name – a condition which obtained throughout large areas of Europe until well into the Middle Ages and even beyond. But they illustrate not so much a constant struggle between Christianity and magic and the old religion, as the interpenetration of Christian life by attitudes towards nature and divinity, which did not substantially alter after the community's conversion. Thus, nature and human beings were conceived as existing symbiotically, the one influencing the other in an existence of mutual participation under divine direction. Hence the belief that human ritual actions could affect the weather or the natural potency of herbs, a belief which could be and was interpreted by Christian authorities as cooperation with undesirable spiritual (i.e. demonic) forces.

Non-Christian belief and practice, then, could also co-exist with Christianity in a state of mutual misapprehension. How, for example, did missionaries convey their particular concept of 'God' or 'sin' or 'penitence' or 'salvation' to peoples whose languages they may not have spoken and whose religious vocabulary almost certainly did not express similar – let alone the same – notions about divinity, creation, and the relationship of human beings therewith? Misunderstanding, ignorance, adaptation are all likely to have played a part in altering many a person's grasp of what his priest was telling him. Hence, perhaps, the Church's condemnation of such beliefs as that which maintained that Satan was the cause of lightning or thunder or storms or droughts[27], or that the vestments worn by priests would put out fires[28]. Nor was it always the case that the laity received adequate instruction. It was said during the trial of Saint Joan of Arc in 1431 that she had not been properly educated or instructed in the faith, but had been under the influence of old women in Domrémy, who were imbued with the knowledge of incantations and divinations, and had passed on their beliefs and expertise to Joan. Indeed, even her own godmother – a woman, let us remember, whose duties included helping to ensure that Joan was brought up a good Catholic – told her much local lore about those spirits or *daimones* known as 'fairies', whom the clerics at Joan's trial not unexpectedly regarded as evil spirits and re-interpreted as such.

This gallimaufry of religious and cultural beliefs, however, was by no means confined to the laity. Priests were perfectly prepared both to make use of magical practitioners and to practise themselves. Toledo (633) makes the first point explicit:

If a bishop or priest or deacon or anyone belonging to holy orders is discovered consulting magicians, diviners who interpret thunder and lightning, people who divine by inspiration (and especially those who interpret the flight of birds), those who cast lots, those who profess any such skill, or anyone practising any similar act: let his punishment be loss of rank and confinement in a monastery where he may expiate by perpetual penitence the crime of sacrilege he has incurred.

But several Councils also addressed the problem of priest-magicians. Agda (506) issued a blanket condemnation of such people; the practice of mingling milk and honey with the eucharistic wine – clearly connected with pagan offerings to the spirits of the dead – was forbidden more than once[29]; priests were also forbidden to seek to punish God by stripping the altars and closing churches when they had some kind of grievance[30], or to say a Requiem Mass for a living person with the intention of bringing about his or her death[31]. Even Popes, it seems, were not immune from accusations of working magic, for the Council of Brixen (1080), inspired, it is true, by the political considerations of some of its members, charged Gregory VII not only with sacrilege and heresy, but also with being an open user of divination and an interpreter of dreams, as well as practising necromancy with the aid of a divinatory spirit; and biased though these charges may have been, there would have been no point in anyone's bringing them had there not been a good chance that they would be believed by a substantial number of people.

So it is worth noting that witches, magicians, diviners, and all the other practitioners of any of the occult sciences did not exist on the margins of society; nor were they confined to a particular group by virtue of their age, their sex, or their education. Anyone at all, cleric or lay, might practise magic in some form at one time or another. We should also put aside the modern habit of drawing strict boundaries between magic, religion, and the natural sciences. Parents with a sick child, for example, were perfectly capable of offering prayers for the child's recovery, turning to the priest for exorcism if the illness were of a kind which warranted that assistance, and seeking the help of an apothecary or amateur herbalist for infusions or poultices whose ingredients might or might not be gathered in accordance with astrological calculations, and put together and administered to the accompaniment of prayers or magical formulae chanted or whispered, or indeed to the accompaniment of both. Magic, it should be emphasized, was not an exotic recourse to which people turned when religion or 'science' in the form of medicine had failed or seemed to fail them. It was a perfectly valid extra or alternative way of seeking to exercise power or tap into the hidden forces of creation for one's personal benefit, even if the official line of both Church and state declared that magic was a dubious activity because of its association with evil spirits and was therefore best left alone. In practice, however, those same officials might well ignore their own prohibitions and behave as everyone else. For no one questioned the possible reality of at least some of the effects of magic. It was the danger to soul and body, which lay inherent in that reality, of which Church and state were afraid; hence their condemnations, decrees, and punishments.

So what made a 'witch' a witch (as opposed to an amateur herbalist, for example, or a heretic, or a scold) is difficult to define. Indeed, in relation to the period we are discussing, it is impossible to define, and it should be noted that none of the legislation of the time attempted to do so. Offenders were designated offenders by virtue of doing certain things or wearing certain objects declared by the legislation to be condemned or forbidden. They were not defined as offenders because they practised a crime which was then described in legal terminology. For all practical purposes, therefore, the 'witch' had not yet been invented. There were only practitioners of various kinds of magic (as the diverse Latin terms make clear), both male and female, who could belong to any rank of ecclesiastical or lay society, and whose actions might or might not bring them within the compass of canon or secular law, depending on external factors which were usually local but could, from time to time, be more general.

One general factor, perhaps the most important, which was liable to influence both ecclesiastical and state authority in relation to magic was the ever-present problem of heresy. Deviation from doctrinal orthodoxy had been fought by the Church ever since its earliest years, and it was therefore inevitable that it would take a dim view of any manifestations of 'magic' which it itself did not approve or control. Thus, for example, Christian prayers offered with a view to affecting the weather were approved; pagan prayers and rituals offered to the same end were not.[32] So magic and heresy were almost bound to be perceived as two sides of the same coin. This can be seen as early as the summer of 368 when Priscillian, the heterodox bishop of Avila, was tried on charges of heresy and maleficent magic (*maleficium*), found guilty, and put to death, largely as a result of his magical activities. Under the court's interrogation, it emerged that Priscillian had taught a doctrine not unlike Manichaeism, in that he distinguished between the creation of human souls created by God and the creation of their bodies by the Devil, thus reflecting that elevation of Satan into a quasi-divine entity and opponent of God which lay at the heart of Manichee teaching. His dualism remained a constant problem for Christian theology into and beyond the Middle Ages. The heretics might have different names at different times – Paulicians, Bogomils, Cathars – but the central question they raised always boiled down to the same thorny point: exactly how powerful was Satan?

Nevertheless, although the official perception of magic might tend to be that it was tainted with heresy, that consideration alone was not sufficient to create the kind of witch whose activities we saw described by Martín del Rio at the start of the previous chapter. Individuals were constantly falling foul of some kind of law which forbade them to practise magic or divination, but except in rare instances such as the deliberate Imperial persecution of the mid-fourth century, they do not seem to have suffered in appreciable numbers drawn from a relatively small region or even single city as victims of an officially-inspired climate of hatred or suspicion. Nor, indeed, was the Church responsible for that fourth-century pogrom. Capital severity, as we have seen, rested with the state. The Church tended rather to seek to administer spiritual cures for what it perceived as spiritual illnesses, and in 1320 the inquisitor Bernardo Gui, provided a standard example of abjuration for anyone who had confessed to or been found guilty of actively participating in magical operations:

I, _____, of such and such a place and such and such a diocese, having been brought before the tribunal, in the presence of you, _____, such and such an inquisitor, do abjure all errors and heresies raising themselves up against the Catholic faith of our Lord Jesus Christ; and in particular I abjure all baptizing of images or any other non-rational objects, and all re-baptizing of people who have been duly and validly baptized already. I abjure any form of divination [*sortilegium*] or harmful magic worked or brought about with or at the expense of the sacred body of Christ, or with baptismal oil, or any holy oil which has been blessed. I abjure all divination and invocation of evil spirits, especially when it is accompanied by worship or honour shown to them or required by them, or homage done to them or required by them; or by any kind of sacrifice or offering of anything made to them by way of sacrifice or offering. I abjure the art and method of making images from lead or wax or any other material in order to bring about illicit effects... I abjure every kind of damnable sorcery [*sortilegium*], especially those which are prescribed for obtaining illicit or harmful effects. I promise and swear that I shall, as far as lies in my power, seek out, uncover, and reveal to inquisitors and secular officials wherever and whenever I may know that some person or persons is or are doing any of the aforesaid operations. I swear and promise to save myself and maintain the Catholic faith.

Practica inquisitionis haereticae pravitatis

This marriage of magic and heresy had important conse-quences. The more closely the two were associated, the more it was likely that official perceptions of magic would resemble official perceptions of heresy. It would be seen, not as hitherto a loose diversity of questionable activities which far too many depraved or foolish individuals persisted in doing for their own selfish ends, but more as an organized movement with its own quasi-theology and liturgy, a distorted mirror of the true faith and the true Church, with its own god, its own angels, its own 'miracles', and its own worshippers. Once perceived this way, the impulse to uproot it, as heresy was to be uprooted, with the help of secular authorities doing their pious duty, became potentially very strong. Thus, in 1437, Pope Eugenius IV issued a bull addressed to all inquisitors, deploring the fact that so many people were practising various forms of magic, worshipping evil spirits, and making pacts with them. In consequence of this, he said, these people were to be arrested, brought before inquisito-rial tribunals and, with the assistance of the local bishops, tried in accordance with canon law, after which they were to be punished. If necessary, the Pope added, the secular authorities should be called on to render their assistance.

Matters had now begun to reach the stage where the witch of the Sabbat could begin to emerge, although the ground for the details of her flight thither and her behaviour when she got there had been laid a long time before the fifteenth century. In c.1115, for example, Guibert of Nogent recorded in his autobiography *Monodiae* (Solitary Songs) details of the behaviour of certain heretics from Soissons. They would meet, he said, in underground chambers where they would light candles and then, coming up behind a woman who was lying upon her stomach with her naked buttocks on view for everyone to see, they would 'present the candles to her' (by which Guibert probably meant they inserted them briefly into her anus). After these ritual acts, the candles were extinguished, everyone shouted 'Chaos!' and indiscriminate sexual intercourse took place. Any babies which might result from this copulation were then brought to another meeting and thrown from one person to another through the flames of a large fire until the child was dead, after which its body was reduced to ashes, made into bread, and eaten as a kind of blasphemous sacrament.[33]

These details (by no means unique, for they had long been told of all kinds of heretics and, in the early days, of Christians themselves), were adapted with only certain changes to give a picture of witches' Sabbats, which rapidly became the norm. By the beginning of the fifteenth century, for example, the heretical sect known as 'Waldensians' or 'Vaudois' had become identified with sorcerers and witches, and *Vauderie* and *Vaudoiserie* were used as synonyms of 'sorcery' or 'witchcraft'; thus amalgamation of the notion of heresy with the notion of magic was complete

– and with magic, it seems, as a whole, although the emphasis did tend to be upon its maleficent operations.

La Vauderye de Lyonois en brief, a selection of extracts made in c.1460 from the interrogations and trials of some Waldensians, shows clearly how propaganda against heretics and the description of witches meeting at a Sabbat have merged into a single picture. The Vaudois, we are told, leave their houses at night, with Satan leading the way. They are drawn from every rank of society and come long distances to attend their diabolical convention. Some of the Vaudois follow him on foot, others on the back of a malignant spirit, others astride a stick which they ride as though it were a horse. Sometimes the Devil disguises himself as an animal – a goat, a huge fox, a dog, a ram, a wolf, a cat, a badger – but always in a form which is filthy, disgusting, and vile. Sometimes he appears to his sectaries in the ghastly form of a black, loathsome man entirely covered with hair.

He has horns on his head. His face is noticeably long, the face of a monster, gnarled and twisted. His bulging eyes stick out further than those of any known animal, and they are always shooting flames and sparks, and swivelling round and round. His nose is big and bent back on itself; his ears are wide and extend upwards a long way and spit fire from their tips; his mouth is open and stretches wide in a curve from ear to ear; his tongue extends a long way from his mouth; his chin is monstrously elongated and curves back in terrifying fashion as far as each cheek; his neck cannot be measured, for it is either so long that it stretches in a way which is dreadful to see, or excessively short, so that it appears to be sticking his head to his shoulder-blades.

Once Satan's devotees have arrived at the Sabbat (here called a 'synagogue'), they worship their master by prostrating themselves or kneeling down before him as suppliants. Each person joins his or her hands together and claps (presumably either by keeping the heels of the hands touching, and clapping with the fingers, or, more likely because of the reference to supplication, by interlacing the fingers and knocking the heels of the hands together in a curious parody of prayer and applause). After this, they kiss the Devil all over his body, including his buttocks. The work of the Sabbat consists of the sectaries renouncing the Christian faith together with all its sacraments and symbols, blaspheming against Jesus and the Virgin Mary, singing to the sound of a muffled trumpet or the bagpipes, and then indulging in brutish anal copulation. Yet there is no chance for enjoyment in any of these activities, for everything takes place in an atmosphere of the greatest terror.

Their blasphemy and singing accomplished, the Vaudois eat and drink together, although the meat is uncooked, glutinous, and filthy. Even the bread smells bad. Then they are subjected to an intense examination, accompanied by torture, concerning all the malefices they have done, after which Satan instructs them in further works of harmful magic. These include sprinkling magical powders on people's food or drink with a view to making them ill, causing pregnant women to miscarry, snatching babies from their cradles or even their mothers' laps, and secretly suffocating them. Some of the Vaudois confess to collecting herbs and putting them to maleficent uses; others to using ointments, needles, bracelets, or keys as instruments of their evil-doing; others to working harmful magic through images made from wax or lead. 'All this and much else,' says the document by way of a conclusion, 'may be found in the confessions of the Lyonnais Vaudois who have been examined by inquisitors'.

But if the Sabbat could be related to anti-heretic propaganda, the witches' flight thither had other, folkloric roots. The *locus classicus* for a description of something similar is to be found in the *Canon Episcopi,* a piece of canon law dating from *c.*906.

> Certain wicked women turn themselves round to face the other way behind Satan and, led astray by hallucinations and figments of their imaginations created by evil spirits, believe and maintain that during the hours of night they ride upon certain beasts along with Diana (a goddess of the pagans), or with Herodias and an innumerable host of women, traversing many areas of the earth in the silent dead of night; that they obey her commands as though she were their mistress, and that on specific nights they are called to her service.

Now, perhaps the most notable aspect of records concerning the flight, and one which should certainly be kept in mind, is the extensive degree of scepticism which attended them. The *Canon Episcopi* itself calls such stories hallucinations and figments of the imagination, and Burchard of Worms later condemned these and other claims to magical ability, and prescribed a penance of forty days on bread and water for seven consecutive years for anyone admitting to belief in them.[34] In the twelfth century, John of Salisbury, in a passage devoted to dreams and visions, declared that there were some people, driven by their sins and the free rein they gave to their wickedness, who were allowed by God to come to such a pitch of madness that they believed (in the most wretched and most lying manner) that something they were experiencing in spirit was actually happening to them bodily – and he gives as an example attendance at a Sabbat in the train of the pagan goddess Herodias.[35] The Dominican, Jordanes of Bergamo, introduced medical causes into the discussion and in *c.*1460 gave it as his opinion that evil spirits worked upon the witch's humours, stirring them up so that they ascended to the brain and there created all kinds of imaginings which caused the witch to believe that he or she had the power to work all kinds of magic, be transported from place to place, and attend the Sabbat where he or she would worship the Devil.[36]

Despite these and similar doubts, however, the story of witches' flights had a certain allure. Thus in the mid-thirteenth century, Thomas of Cantimpré recounted the anecdote of a nobly-born girl who, at the same hour each night, was carried away bodily by evil spirits, and although her brother, a monk, did his best to prevent this from happening by grasping her firmly in his arms, as soon as the hour arrived she disappeared.[37] In the early fifteenth century, Johannes Nider, whose *Formicarius* is an important repository of key ideas in the development of the theory of witches' behaviour, was told about the experience of a fellow Dominican who arrived at a village to be confronted by a woman who claimed that at night she flew with Diana[38]: and although neither Nider nor his informant believed her story, the fact of its being told is enough to indicate that belief in such flight was still common. Then in *c.*1440 we find Martin le Franc, secretary to the anti-Pope Felix V, writing a long poem, *Champion des Dames*, in which two speakers exchange views on witches and their wicked practices. One of them describes women going to the Sabbat on foot or on sticks, 'flying through the air like birds', and the manuscript illustrates the point with two marginal miniatures showing one woman astride a besom and the other riding a long, stout staff. Significantly, they fly under the heading 'Vaudoises'. It may also be worth bearing in mind, when considering this notion of flight, that the constant use of the Latin word *strix* (owl or witch) or its vernacular derivatives would have been likely to underline, if only subliminally, the perceived connection between flying and those accused of being witches.

These developments can also be followed in other examples of contemporary art. A fresco from southern Tyrol, dated to the eleventh or twelfth century, shows the Devil, or at least an evil spirit, riding upon a boar in the full tilt of a hunt – an image which is transmuted about a century later in one of the sculptures from the west front of Lyons cathedral, depicting a witch perched on the back of a goat and holding by its back legs her captured prey, some kind of cat. There are also stories (or perhaps versions of a particular story) to be found in Vincent de Beauvais and William of Malmesbury about a woman being carried off to Hell by an evil spirit astride a horse, and Olaus Magnus's *History of the Peoples of the North* has a woodcut to illustrate it (plate 7). So it is not difficult to see how the amalgamation of tales and images relating to demonic hunts and women transported by spirits on the back of an animal produced, at least in one of its phases, one of the standard pictures of the witch on her way to the Sabbat; and when it comes to flying on staves or broomsticks, we have a twelfth-century German mural which shows the goddess Frigga being transvected in just such a fashion, and an interesting fifteenth-century miniature depicting a witch on the back of a demonic creature, with two evil spirits in attendance, one of whom is brandishing what looks like a diminutive besom.

By the second half of the fifteenth century, then, there had come into existence a notion of the witch not completely at variance with earlier conceptions and models of the magical operator, but one which tended to concentrate on certain newly developed theatrical (as opposed to everyday magical) aspects of her behaviour: one says 'her' because in much of the literature which was beginning to specialize in discussion of these aspects, the witch now seems to have been visualized more or less as distinctively female. What is more, her activities were described as those of a person who was less a depraved individual and more a willing member or adherent of an organized anti-Christian sect of Devil-worshippers whose aim was to help Satan corrupt the society of the faithful and thereby swell the ranks of the damned in Hell, and one work in particular summarized and made vivid the various strands which went to make up this relatively new picture – at once the most notorious and the most peculiar of all the demonologies – Heinrich Krämer's *Malleus Maleficarum*.

CHAPTER THREE

A Plague of Witches

M*alleus Maleficarum* (The Hammer of Women who work Harmful Magic) is perhaps the best-known treatise on witches and witchcraft because it is so often referred to and quoted from, but the general reader may not appreciate what an unusual – not to say strange – work it is in certain respects. Commonly attributed to two Dominicans, Heinrich Krämer (or Institoris) and Jakob Sprenger, it was written principally by the former and printed first in 1487. It begins with a confidence trick, for the work is prefaced by a Bull of Innocent VIII issued to Institoris and Sprenger on 9 December 1484, and its presence at the start of the *Malleus* is meant to suggest that the Pope was favourably inclined to the prosecution of witches undertaken by the two inquisitors, and that he approved their methods of proceeding. In fact, the Bull was granted in response to a request by Institoris for Papal support against certain regional authorities in Germany whom Institoris perceived as hostile to his inquisitorial practices – 'Let the preacher be armed against certain arguments of laymen, and even of some learned men, who deny, up to a certain point, that there are witches,' as he recorded later[1] – and there is no indication that the Pope was exercised more than any of his predecessors about magic or witchcraft, witches or magicians, or even that he saw a copy of the *Malleus* when it appeared two or three years later. The Bull, then, has no direct connection with Institoris's treatise.

It may be divided into three parts: firstly, the Pope is concerned about the spread of heresy, especially in certain parts of Germany where apostates have succumbed to the wiles of evil spirits and practise multifarious forms of maleficent magic (none of which, incidentally, include flight to the Sabbat or the Sabbat itself); secondly, Institoris and Sprenger are inquisitors in those areas but are being hindered in their work by certain over-officious clerics and lay people who question the existence of maleficent magic in their territories, and the authority of Institoris and Sprenger to deal with it; thirdly, therefore the Pope gives details of what Institoris and Sprenger are authorized to do, and insists that there shall be no more obstacles put in their way. So while the Bull acknowledges the widespread existence of magic-as-apostasy and magic-as-heresy in a number of German regions, its principal theme is actually political, an assertion of Papal authority over local officials who have ventured to question it in the persons of two of its representatives already authorized to root out that heretical depravity to which the Pope refers.

Now, Institoris had been one of the principals in two trials for witchcraft: the first in Ravensburg in October 1484, the second (a series of judicial processes rather than a single trial) in Brixen between August 1485 and February 1486. At Ravensburg, Institoris was successful in prosecuting two women, but at Brixen he ran into difficulties. The local bishop was sceptical of the claims made by complainants against a large number of people from his diocese – 'the illusions of evil spirits', he called them, quite after the style of the *Canon Episcopi* – and he was also of the opinion that Institoris was exceeding his brief and authority in the manner he was conducting investigations. One can see his point. The episode began with fifty suspects, forty-eight of whom were women. Most came from the local peasantry, while the witnesses against them were drawn from a much wider social spectrum. After the initial interrogations were over, it was decided in October 1485 that charges would be brought against seven women who were thereupon imprisoned for the duration of the rest of the proceedings. Witnesses said they had been bewitched by a remarkable diversity of magical instruments including powders, human and animal hairs, bones from unbaptized babies, shavings of paint from religious pictures, and Jewish faeces. The Devil was invoked during these magical operations. One witch was said to have instructed young people in the arts of love-magic and malefice, and details were provided of how a witch magically stole milk from her neighbour's cow and of the counter-magic one could use to make her reveal herself.

Institoris, it appears, was particularly interested in pursuing certain lines of questioning. He wanted to elucidate the part played by Satan in these magical workings; he was keen to discover details about the unguents supposedly made from babies' bodies; and he pressed one witch in particular, Helena Scheuberin, about her sexual practices and her moral standing in her community. The bishop of Brixen, however, objected strongly to this tack and Institoris's fellow-commissioners agreed, insisting that the woman's sexual life was irrelevant to the charges in hand. There followed a long period of judicial argument about Institoris's methods and competence until finally his opponents gained their point. Institoris was overruled, the trial was postponed indefinitely, and the women were released from prison. But the bishop continued his hostility toward Institoris personally, and at last in February 1486, he advised him to leave Innsbruck because (or at least so he maintained) he could no longer guarantee the inquisitor's safety. Institoris was therefore obliged to make a humiliating retreat, but the episode simply made him more determined to pursue his task of uncovering and eliminating heretics, and witch-heretics in particular. Hence the writing and publication of *Malleus Maleficarum*.

The general form and content of the book is as follows. It is divided into three parts: the first proffers a theological view of magic, which is intended to underpin the other two; the second describes the activities of workers of harmful magic, both male and female; and the third sets out in some detail the judicial procedure to be adopted against those who have been arrested and accused of witchcraft.

Part I starts with the round declaration that witches do exist and that Catholics must accept this. The Devil is an essential component of the process of working any kind of magic, and yet none of this activity can happen or have any validity unless God is agreeable to it and gives his permission. This he does either to punish sinners, or to test the faith of believers, or to make matters worse for the witches by letting them bewitch people who are entirely innocent. Witchcraft, says Institoris, is increasing at the present time because of human wickedness and not (as some people try to maintain), because of adverse astral influences, the conjunction of Jupiter and Saturn, or the appearance of comets. Human wickedness, however, is not sufficient in itself to explain the phenomenon. For that one needs to bear in mind the active cooperation of Satan who has his own malicious reasons for encouraging it.

Women are especially addicted to all forms of superstitious behaviour and therefore become witches much more readily than men, because they are morally and intellectually weak and have insatiable sexual appetites. Hence, they can sway men's minds through their excessive emotionalism, render men impotent, and even trick them into thinking they have lost their genitals altogether. Women are also willing to have sexual intercourse with evil spirits in the form of *incubi* (originally spirits who settled on people while they were asleep and caused them to suffocate), but any children born of such a union are actually the offspring of another human being, because the *incubi* cannot generate semen themselves, but must steal it from a man and then insert it into the woman at the appropriate moment. Witches are idolaters and apostates, their guilt is enormous, even greater than that of evil spirits, and sceptics must be left in no doubt that this is so.

Part II is divided into two. The first section has as its object a description of the range of magical offences committed by witches, but begins with the interesting observation that there are certain groups of people who are immune to witchcraft: (a) judicial officers; (b) those who benefit from the Church's exorcisms by being sprinkled with holy water, or carrying candles blessed on the Feast of the Purification of the Virgin or palm leaves blessed on Palm Sunday; and (c) those who are blessed in various ways by good angels. Subversion of other, susceptible individuals is possible under various circumstances: if someone has suffered material loss in some way, or if someone has made the mistake of consulting a witch, asking her or him for a magical favour, and has been inveigled into promising to return the favour by dishonourable or blasphemous actions during Mass. In the case of a young woman, the opening to demonic temptation may lie in her carnal desires, or in her guilt after copulating with and being abandoned by a lover, and perhaps in her wish to be revenged upon him.

Next Institoris gives a series of commentaries on a familiar list of magical activities attributed to witches: making a pact with an evil spirit, being transported through the air, causing impotence in men and otherwise interfering with the bonds of marriage, changing men into animals, causing demonic possession or physical illness, killing children, harming animals, and changing the course of the weather. None of these is new. They may all be found in earlier writers who touch upon or discuss magic, and indeed they are pretty well a reiteration of the list of magical activities given by Pope Innocent VIII in his Bull of 1484.

The novelty Institoris does provide for his readers in this second part of the *Malleus* is his frequent use of illustrative anecdotes. Scholarly works, then as now, supported their arguments and contentions with references to earlier literature, and it is a commonplace of medieval and early modern academic works that they will not distinguish between genres – history, poetry, legislation, religious texts, romances are all equally grist to the mill. Nor will they distinguish between chronological periods. A quotation from a second century BC Roman writer will be made to rub shoulders quite happily with a chronicler of the thirteenth century AD, for example, their evidence equally timeless and equally valid. But what Institoris does is to introduce contemporary instances as a way of giving extra immediacy to his argument: 'In the same year I started writing this book, a certain devout woman…', 'I know a stranger in the diocese of Augsburg…', 'Another young woman living in the diocese of Strasburg confessed to one of us...'. Academic evidence, these anecdotes seem to suggest, is indeed available and compelling, but up-to-date, and in some cases personal, experience underlines the immediacy of the problem, and perhaps looks to quicken the fear of his readers that they and their community cannot regard themselves as immune from this moral plague.

The *Malleus* has been closely identified with misogyny – without, it should be said, much justification: it is no more biased in that way than other works of the period – so it is interesting to find that he devotes the final chapter of this first section to men who practise certain specialized forms of magic. He discusses three types: 'archers' who shoot arrows at a crucifix during Mass on Good Friday in order magically to acquire greater skill in their shooting at other times; those who use incantations and charms to render certain weapons harmless if used against them, and blasphemously mutilate a crucifix in accordance with the part of their own body they wish to be protected; and then those who enchant weapons so that they can walk on them with bare feet, and perform similar wonderful tricks. (The 'archers' remind one of pictures in the *Chroniche* of the fourteenth-century historian Giovanni Sercambi, showing angels of death infecting individuals with plague by shooting them with arrows; and Ulrich Molitor's witchcraft treatise, *De lamiis et phitonicis mulieribus* [Women who are Witches and Foretellers of the Future], published in 1489, has a woodcut depicting a witch crippling a man magically by firing arrows into his foot [plate 8].) There are princes, says Institoris darkly, who make use of such magicians, especially in time of war, and traders and merchants frequently wear charms and amulets which they have provided. But no one, however exalted in station – and here Institoris specifies 'bishops' and 'rulers', with evident reference to those who had thwarted him in Innsbruck – is above being punished for aiding and abetting the crime of witchcraft, and ought to pay the appropriate penalties.

This sidelong and rather peculiar glance at men completed (peculiar because he ignores far more common types of male magician), Institoris now turns to discuss the various ways in which maleficent magic may lawfully be countered. One must not use witchcraft to undo witchcraft, he says, but rely upon the effective remedies provided by the Church: prayer, exorcism, its sacraments, and sacramentals.

Finally, in Part III, Institoris goes into considerable detail about the available judicial procedures for interrogating and trying those accused of witchcraft. Witchcraft sometimes involves heresy, sometimes not. But regardless of the presence or absence of actual heresy, anyone who practises magic of any kind whatever is liable to be tried in an Inquisitorial court which may depute other people, such as the local bishop, to act in its stead; and because witches commit crimes with civil consequences – murder, for example, or destruction of goods or property – the civil courts, too, may properly try such cases and inflict capital punishment where this is the appropriate penalty. Once information has been laid against someone and a full written account of the accusations obtained, witnesses must be sworn and examined. The names of witnesses are not to be concealed unless there is reason to believe that the witnesses will be put in danger by publication of their identities, and the evidence of those who are at mortal enmity with the accused is not admissible.

This stage of the process completed, the accused is to be arrested and either granted bail or put into prison in accordance with the usual local practice. If the defendant asks for a defence-advocate, the judge will appoint someone suitable, 'an honourable man to whom no element of suspicion is attached', and if the advocate thinks the case worth fighting – in other words, if it is neither unjust, nor obvious to all that the defendant is guilty – he may undertake the defence. (It is sometimes forgotten that accused witches were not always left to the judgement of an entirely hostile court. The conduct of witch-craft cases in Scotland, for example, as we shall see in the next chapter, always presumed the active presence of a defence-advocate for anyone, regardless of wealth or social status, who might find her or himself accused of this crime.)

Institoris now passes to the question of torture, an aspect of witchcraft trials often illustrated by carefully selected horrors without much – or sometimes any – attempt to explain why and how it was employed. Let us begin with the simple fact that torture was likely to be used in a whole range of criminal offences. It was not a device reserved exclusively for women or for witches. Secondly, let us acknowledge that practising magic of all kinds was designated a criminal offence by a large number of legislatures and that in consequence those brought into court were regarded as criminals, just as were those accused of murder or treason or any other offence carrying the death penalty.

The special status of witchcraft as a *crimen exceptum*, a crime for which the normal rules of gathering evidence were suspended or relaxed, must not, of course, be forgotten or pass without expla-nation. The basis for regarding it as such lay in the secretive nature of the offence which meant that, unlike murder where a dead body pointed clearly to both the fact and the type of the crime, any connection between, say, the death of a child, the loss of a cow's milk, or the sudden onset of illness, was a matter of inference. Some inferences were strong, others weak, and taken together they could build a strong case for the accused to refute and explain. But these inferences (*indicia*), which were all witnesses could offer, were not enough by themselves to convict someone accused of this capital offence. In order to be certain of the accused's guilt, a confession was required, the very first point made and emphasized by Institoris at this point in his discussion[2]. But if the confession can be elicited by means other than torture, they should be used. Institoris suggests that the rigours of imprisonment may be sufficient to bring this about; or the witch may be allowed to receive visitors who should try to persuade her or him to confess. Threats and promises may also be employed, although the promises may be misleading as when, for example, the witch is promised her or his life in return for a full confession, but not told that compliance will result in life imprisonment rather than liberty. Some witches, he observes, confess readily to their crimes; others do not; and some commit suicide after they have confessed. These various reactions indicate the degrees of control exercised over them by the evil spirit.

If no confession can be drawn by any of the devices he has mentioned, Institoris says the judge may then proceed to sentence the witch to be tortured. Torture is to be light in the first instance and every precaution taken in advance to make sure the accused is not wearing any protective amulets or other magical devices whereby the effects of torture may be nullified. A full written record of the torture session is to be kept, and if the witch confesses at this point, she or he is to be taken to another room and questioned again in case the confession was produced merely by the pain and stress of the ordeal. Should no such confession be forthcoming, however, the witch may be re-tortured and the severity of the torture increased. But throughout this period, all the other methods Institoris has mentioned and outlined should continue to be used, and the judge should scrutinize the defendant for particular signs from which guilt may be inferred, such as the known inability of a witch to shed tears of repentance. While they are engaged in their duties, Institoris adds, the judges and other court officials must take care not to allow the witch to touch them or look at them before they look at her, for fear she or he may still retain sufficient magical power to bewitch them; and the officials are also advised to carry on their persons sacramentals, such as salt blessed on Palm Sunday, so that they may benefit from this authorized and legitimate form of protection.

Next, Institoris turns briefly to a very particular question. Can a secular judge allow a witch to submit her or himself to purgation as a means of testing her or his guilt or innocence? Purgation was an old-fashioned method of applying for God's judgement in one's case and there were several kinds, for example, trial by combat or duel, red-hot iron, and boiling or freezing water. If the accused could withstand the pain of the iron or the boiling water and if, after a certain number of days, his or her flesh had healed without scarring, these circumstances were taken as a sign from God that the person was innocent. During the twelfth century, however, purgation had started to fall out of favour with the Church on the grounds that it smacked of blasphemy, and the old Roman style of endeavouring to uncover the truth by questioning (*interrogatio*) had come to take its place in ecclesiastical courts and then, gradually, in criminal courts as well. The method of testing a suspected witch by swimming her – if she sank she was innocent, if she floated she was guilty – which lasted in some places well into the eighteenth century, was also a type of purgation, although many Catholic writers on witchcraft, such as the Jesuit Martín del Rio, heartily condemned the practice. Indeed, Institoris, having raised the question of purgation and secular judges, denounced it as unlawful and pointed out that in any case one could not rely on its efficacy because the Devil was capable of looking after his own and so rendering the exercise useless.

The treatise ends with a series of practical questions relating to the passing of a sentence and the matter of appeals. What should a judge do in cases where someone has been accused on light suspicion, or strong suspicion, or very grave suspicion? What happens if the accused has confessed to heresy but shows no repentance, or is a relapsed heretic who is now penitent? What is to be done when the defendant has been convicted but continues to deny everything, or has managed to flee the court after a guilty verdict? What should one do in the case of someone accused by a convicted witch, or who is an 'archer' magician? How should the judge deal with witches who enter an appeal, and how is he to treat appeals which are (a) frivolous, (b) legitimate, or (c) right and proper? The answers to all these questions demonstrate the essential point of the *Malleus*, to assist future inquisitors and judges in the proper conduct and resolution of investigations into and trials of this exceptionally appalling and very difficult crime.

Now, modern discussions of the *Malleus* sometimes take the line that it is a bigoted and therefore fatally flawed, not to say dangerous work. Certainly its argumentation is muddled and frequently raises questions which are not followed through. Take, as one example, the immunity of judges. Institoris specifically says that judicial officials cannot be harmed by witches once they have been arrested, and yet he also says that judges are susceptible to enchantment and should therefore carry or wear sacramentals by way of protection. Both statements cannot be right, but Institoris does not seem to notice their incompatibility. It is also often assumed that the *Malleus* demonstrates misogyny to an unusual degree. Certainly there is an edge to the whole work which is likely to belong to Institoris. His choice of title, for example, is significant. *Malleus* means 'hammer' or 'maul' and medieval scholars would have been well aware from their reading of Ovid that in Classical Latin the word referred not only to an instrument for knocking in nails or pegs, but also to a ritual object used to stun a sacrificial victim before the creature received its death-blow. Clearly Institoris was thinking of this usage when he coined his title – the other, craft meaning does not make sense in the context – with the 'hammer' representing himself and, indeed, any other judge who might oversee the trial of a witch. It is a remarkably violent image and one which, quite contrary we may suppose to Institoris's intention, casts the witch in the part of the innocent sacrificial animal.

The other word of the title, *Maleficarum*, refers quite specifically to female workers of harmful magic. *Malefici* (masculine) and *maleficae* (feminine) are the words Institoris most commonly employs to designate 'witches', quite in line with the regular usage of both this and the earlier period. But his treatise makes it clear that, archer-magicians apart, his principal targets are the female practitioners of magic, and herein he follows the growing trend of the fourteenth and fifteenth centuries to view witches as women rather than men. The perception coincides, to some extent, with emerging official hostility to the diversity of forms of religious life for women at this time. Suspicion of visionary or prophetic women – and one thinks, among others, of Saint Bridget of Sweden, Saint Catherine of Siena, and Saint Joan of Arc – reflected the deep uncertainty of theologians over how to interpret female manifestations of contact with powers other than human. The potential female saint began to seem in many ways rather like the new model of a witch. Saint Catherine of Siena, for example, received the stigmata, replicas of the five wounds of Christ, upon her body; a witch received marks from the Devil or from the *incubi* who had sexual intercourse with her. Saint Catherine, just like the witch, was visited by evil spirits; she, however, resisted their seductions, the witch did not. The intellectual ambience of the period, then, coincided with what appears to have been Institoris's personal animus against women to produce a title whose violence is unique among the titles of treatises on witchcraft.

This is the book's first peculiarity. Its second lies in the single-minded, blinkered assumption that those who are accused of witchcraft and brought to trial will be found guilty. In practice, as even a cursory glance at surviving records will show, large numbers were declared innocent by the courts and set at liberty. But Institoris will, apparently, have none of it. He sees the universe in a very particular light. Its functioning is more or less controlled by Satan and a host of evil spirits, and although God is evidently master of creation and everything which happens, good or ill, happens by his permission, the degree of freedom allowed the Devil is alarming. Hence, therefore, Institoris's conviction that one must be ruthless in seeking out and destroying the Devil's servants upon earth, those being all practitioners of magic, but witches – practitioners of deliberately harmful magic – especially.

Thirdly, the book contains a number of surprises, not in what it says but in what it omits. The *Malleus* is the first comprehensive work on witchcraft, intended both to explain the phenomenon theologically and to advise ministers of justice how best to deal with it. During the previous century at least, as we have seen, there had been growing a version of witches' behaviour which had them flying through the air, attending Sabbats, and worshipping the Devil – behaving in many ways, in fact, like a deliberately organized counter-Church. Yet Institoris deals with none of this. He makes no mention of feasting, sexual orgies, the Devil's mark, the debasing kiss, or personal attendant-demons (familiars), and to that extent one might be tempted to call his treatise oddly old-fashioned.

But this, I think, would be a mistake. Intellectuals have always run ahead of public opinion, sometimes in a useful direction, sometimes up a cul-de-sac. The Devil-worshipping theory of witches had certainly proved increasingly popular with theologians, and would continue to be so during the sixteenth and seventeenth centuries, drawing into its ambit lawyers and doctors and, to some extent, the common people. But the fact is that a large proportion (the majority) of those accused of witchcraft were actually charged with practising traditional forms of magic – inducing love, curing illness, wreaking harm of various kinds, and so forth – with scarcely a mention of Satan beyond his meeting them once or twice alone, at home or in the country, and persuading them to become his servant. No flying, no Sabbat, no orgy, no acts of communal worship. The idolatry version of witches' activities does appear, of course, but it is more prevalent by and large in witchcraft treatises than in surviving court records, and to that extent the *Malleus* reflects actual court experience of the charges laid against witches, and can thus correctly be described as a practical manual rather than an academic monograph.

Even so, the fourth peculiar fact about it is its lack of lasting effect. To be sure, the book was quoted constantly by subsequent scholars and its initial publishing history – perhaps eight editions before the end of the fifteenth century – suggests that it created something of a sensation in literate circles for a while, although we have no clear notion of how many copies of a book constituted an 'edition' in the fifteenth century. (Between 275 and 300 seems to be a credible figure.) Nevertheless, there was no appreciable increase in the number of prosecutions for witchcraft, except perhaps in the early 1490s in the Rhineland, and so in as far as the *Malleus* was intended to be a clarion call to inquisitors and judges to eradicate the growing menace of diabolism, it largely failed. Intensive prosecution of witches would not occur, in fact, for nearly a century.

◦━✦━◦

Throughout the Middle Ages and well into the early modern period, Europe was troubled at frequent intervals by thoughts of apocalypticism and millenarianism. Both involved the Devil and an end of the world as it had been known until then. Both helped to create recurrent climates of fear in which people might be tempted to seek relief from tension and stress by uncovering scapegoats who would act as diversions of God's wrath and what seemed like the inevitability of universal dissolution. Jews and witches, by reason of their being perceived as enemies of Christ, might serve as just such scapegoats should the need arise.

Apocalypticism takes its name from the last book of the New Testament, the *Apocalypse* or 'unveiling' by Saint John. Interpretation of the book is difficult and its message obscure, for different ages have drawn various meanings from it. Certain passages, however, were seen more or less consistently as prophecies of the end of creation which would be preceded by the birth of a monstrous individual known as the Antichrist, and culminate in the second coming of Jesus Christ to judge all humanity, the dead as well as the living. This Last Judgement would determine who was fit to enter Heaven and remain there with God throughout eternity, and who was to be damned and so remain in Hell. The prospect of eternal damnation was an ever-present possibility for successive congregations, hammered from the pulpit and delineated by artists in ever more horrendously imaginative detail. Judgement Day, however, would not come without warning. Apart from the appearance of Antichrist, there would be wars, famines, and plagues, and above all Satan himself would have leave from God to ravage the world. Saint John was quite clear on this point:

> Then I saw an angel coming down from heaven, holding in his hand the key of the bottomless pit and a great chain. And he seized the dragon, that ancient serpent who is the Devil and Satan, and bound him for a thousand years, and threw him into the pit, and shut it and sealed it over him, that he should deceive the nations no more, till the thousand years were ended. After that he must be loosed for a while.
>
> *Apocalypse* 20.1–3

Thus 'millenarianism' joined hands with apocalyptic ideas. The term refers to the complex of prophecies which grew round contemplation of this thousand-year period mentioned by Saint John, and it became a matter of debate when the thousand years began and therefore when one should calculate its end. Thus, the Franciscan Roger Bacon (*c.*1213–*c.*1291) suggested that the Church encourage a more intensive study of learned literature with a view to determining the date of Antichrist's arrival:

I don't want to speak out of turn, but I do know that if the Church were willing to take another look at the Bible and the holy prophecies, along with the prophecies of the Sibyl, Merlin, Aquila, Sesto, Joachim of Fiore, and many others and, in addition, histories and the books of philosophers: and if she were to urge people to investigate the ways of astrology, then one might discover a faint but adequate notion (or, it would be more correct to say, a certainty), about when Antichrist is due to appear.

Opus Maius, part 4, 'Judicial Astrology'

This was written in the mid-thirteenth century, a period when flagellants roamed various countrysides, whipping their flesh and staging theatrical, sometimes violent spectacles as a call to general repentance in preparation for the imminent Day of Judgement. Joachim of Fiore, the Franciscan to whom Bacon made allusion, prophesied that Antichrist was about to initiate his reign and that after him a third age of renewal of creation would begin in about 1260, and only ten years or so before that crucial date, yet another Franciscan composed the famous poem *Dies Irae* (The Day of Anger) which described the terrors which would be attendant on that final day of the world, the day of the second coming and the last judgement.

To be sure, the terror of the moment passed. But it was renewed again and again at later times by what seemed to contemporaries to be signs of the final times. So, between 1306 and 1314, the Order of Knights Templar was attacked and then dissolved amid stories of sexual orgies during initiation ceremonies, and worshipping of the Devil in the guise of a diabolical head. Between 1348 and 1350, Europe was ravaged by various forms of plague known collectively as the 'Black Death'. The disease triggered pogroms of Jews in certain places, and confirmed the notion that Antichrist either had arrived or was about to arrive, and that in consequence the end of everything was imminent, with the Holy Roman Emperor, Frederick II, acting as regent for God with power to reform corruption in the Church. The last decades of the fourteenth century and the opening decades of the next saw a great schism in the Western Church, when the Papacy was removed from Rome to Avignon and rival popes were elected at the same time, each claiming authentic suzerainty. Little wonder, then, that the Dominican Saint Vincent Ferrer (1357-1419) believed his world had entered the final times and wrote a book, *De fine mundi* (The End of the Universe), to give vent to his prophetic fears.

Institoris's conviction during the 1480s that the world was being plagued with witches and that the Devil had received permission to extend his infernal empire upon earth was therefore understandable in the light of apocalyptic terrors and millenarian expectations which had by no means disappeared from Europe, but were indeed all too alive. Astrologers had predicted that 1484 was to be a significant year for humanity, since a conjunction of Jupiter and Saturn would mark the end of an astrological era, and the entry of the sun into the zodiacal house of Aries indicated great changes in religion. Sure enough, it was during the 1480s and 1490s that a Dominican friar, Girolamo Savonarola, prophesied the coming of the kingdom of God and the consequent need for immediate repentance. His personal influence was so dominant in Florence, and popular belief in the truth of what he was saying was so strong there, that the city fell almost entirely under both his spell and his command. Fear of invasion by French troops (part of the complex turmoil of Italian politics during this time), certainly helped to create this particular climate, but war was one of the signs of the last days, as the *Apocalypse* said, and even after the tide had turned against Savonarola and he had been burned as a heretic in 1498, Italian expectations of the end of the world continued to burn, like charcoal in a censer.

In 1501, Botticelli painted his *Mystical Nativity* (plate 10), ostensibly an image of the adoration of the new-born Christ by his Virgin Mother and the shepherds, but actually an embodiment of Savonarola's vision (fuelled by many other millennial prophecies which were continuing to circulate), that a renovation of the Church was about to happen as part of the final times. Botticelli makes his point clear in the message, written in Greek, which is spread across the top of the canvas:

> This picture I, Alessandro, painted at the end of the year 1500 [which is 1501 in our calendar], during the troubles of Italy, in the half-time after the time, during the fulfilment of the eleventh [chapter] of John, during the second woe of the *Apocalypse*, during the loosing of the Devil for three and a half years. Afterwards, according to the twelfth [chapter], he will be chained and we shall see him as in this picture.

Sure enough, only sixteen years later, reformation of the Church did begin, a reformation so violent, it tore the Church apart, disrupted Europe, and set it ablaze with religious wars, thus seeming to confirm that the Apocalypse was really, finally, about to be enacted.

But if the last days were actually in process of happening in the first half of the sixteenth century, where or who was Antichrist? He, after all, was to be the diabolical equivalent of Saint John the Baptist and proclaim Satan's imminent rule. He ought, therefore, to be identifiable. During the early Middle

Ages, Antichrist seemed to be a less specific, or at least more shadowy figure. In *c.*786, for example, Saint Beatus of Liebana expressed the matter thus:

> Antichrist is always overcome by the Church. For it is not, as some people think, that Antichrist will persecute the Church in one particular place, because one might say that Antichrists are everywhere. Antichrist will be the final king and will rule over the whole of creation. He will say he is God, that is, Christ. But in actual fact, Antichrist is hidden in the Church, because he has not yet overtly been given power. But when he does come, he will bring the whole world under his control, as it is said about him in the book of *Job* [21.33]: 'He draws every person behind him, and those before him are without number'.
>
> *In Apocalipsim libri duodecim* 2.83–5

But during the later Middle Ages, heretical movements were quick to identify Antichrist as the current Pope. The Englishman John Wyclif wrote in 1379 that he found it quite probable that the present Pope was the Antichrist described in Scripture – although he was careful to add that just because someone believed one Pope was Antichrist, it did not follow that he had to believe every Pope was Antichrist.[3] The Czech heretic Jan Hus, too, clearly identified the reigning Pope as Antichrist in letters to Christian of Prachatice, written in 1413, and to Wenceslas of Dubá and John of Chlum in June 1415, and it is perhaps no accident that both men were writing at times when there were two Popes simultaneously claiming legitimacy, Urban VI and 'Clement VII' in 1379, and Gregory XIII and 'John XXIII' in 1413–15. But the practice of heretics declaring that Antichrist had arrived and was sitting upon the throne of Saint

Peter in Rome, once established, continued well beyond the initial stages of the Protestant reformation and provided dissidents from Rome with a weapon in their disputational armoury far into the sixteenth century.

We have, then, throughout the Middle Ages, recurrent signs which might be read as fulfilments of those described by the *Apocalypse*, and waves of expectation that the Last Judgement was imminent and that the end of creation (or at least the end of this stage of world history), was about to happen. So if people wanted to seek scapegoats for their fears, as they did during the Black Death by killing large numbers of Jews, it would not have been surprising to see them turn, at any of these critical junctures, against practitioners of magic, especially those wilfully doing harm to their immediate neighbours and the rest of their community. Yet, as we have seen in connection with the later history of the *Malleus Maleficarum*, no such pogrom of witches appears to have happened until the 1580s and '90s. Why, then, did people stay their hands at the end of the fifteenth century, but actively turn them against magical operators a hundred years later?

It cannot really be argued that a combination of apocalypticism, millenarianism, signs, heresy, institutional misogyny, and contingent stress and fear was responsible alone for the intensive outbreak of witch-prosecutions which can be seen in the surviving records of the eighty-year period between *c.*1580 and *c.*1660 in Western Europe. After all, these factors, sometimes with emphasis upon one, sometimes upon another, sometimes on all together, had been prevalent in the history of the West for many, if not most of the preceding centuries. What, then, was different about the situation at the end of the sixteenth century?

One must be careful here not to suggest there may a single reason for what is often called the persecution of witches. Syphilis, hatred of women, climatic change, shifts in the balance of political power, collective psychosis and mass delusion because of peculiarities of diet or ingestion of drugs have all been proposed at one time or another, with hatred of women leading the field as the most popular catch-all explanation. But, just as 'witchcraft' was not a monolithic intellectual or pseudo-religious structure open to a single description, but a portmanteau word capable of holding an extraordinary variety of different beliefs and practices with only their reliance on some kind of preternatural power as a common thread between them, so explanations of why people were accused of practising various forms of magic must take into account time, place, circumstance, sex, personal beliefs, social status, and a dozen other considerations local, national, and international.

By the 1580s, however, it was possible to detect three crucial factors which might be said to have made a difference from the earlier periods. First, when heresy had reared its head before, the Church, by and large, had managed to suppress it. The suppression had not always been easy, nor was it always total, as the survival of Nestorianism and Catharism could testify. Nevertheless, to all intents and appearances – and appearances here mattered very much indeed – the Church seemed to have emerged victorious from each contest with heresy and the leading heresiarchs had often been discredited or even put to death. The advent of Luther and Calvin, however, with their plethora of followers, quickly created a situation beyond the Church's control. Whole regions of Europe fell away from the Church and adhered to the new religionists, and although wars both large and small were fought to overthrow or maintain these new dispositions, heresy in the form of Lutheranism and Calvinism and their many variations did not seem to be conquerable this time.

Secondly, with the Protestant reformation theological speculation over the relationship between the power of God and the power of the Devil became part of the confessional divide. Early in the third century AD, the theologian Lactantius had proposed that the existence of evil was necessary for people's spiritual progress:

> If God has created everything out of consideration for the interests of humankind, why do we also find many things, in the sea and on the land, which are injurious, hostile, and deadly for us? ...When God shaped man in his image (something which was the summit of the divine work of creation), he breathed wisdom into him alone, so that man might subdue everything to his authority and dominion and make use of all the beneficial things in the universe. But God put before him evil things as well as good, because he gave him wisdom whose entire purpose was to distinguish between good and evil... Suppose evil did not exist, no danger, nothing which could hurt humankind: the whole building-block of wisdom would be taken away and humanity would have no need of it at all.
>
> *De ira Dei* 13.9, 13, 16

But herein is raised the thorny question of how far evil may be permitted to extend its influence or rule over human beings, a question which Manichaeism had sought to answer by proposing the existence of two equal gods, one good, one evil, locked in perpetual battle with each other. While this solution, self-evidently, was rejected by orthodox theologians (though not without a struggle, as the case of Saint Augustine bears witness), it left its mark on much subsequent theological controversy, nowhere perhaps more evidently than in matters relating to magic.

To put it in the simplest possible terms, the witchcraft debate saw Catholics and Protestants in agreement about the omnipotence of God, and about the necessity of God's permission before Satan, his evil spirits, and their allies – the operators of magic – could enter into any kind of pact which would produce extraordinary effects and either apparent benefit or overt harm to individuals or communities. Protestants tended then to suggest that, since God was omnipotent, any power exercised within creation by the Devil or any of his adherents must be part of God's overall plan for humanity. Anyone who suffered from the attention of witches or evil spirits must therefore put all his or her trust in God and wait patiently until God chose to limit or end the suffering. Catholics, by way of contrast, tended to lay more emphasis on the active presence of evil in the world and therefore upon the genuine harm done by Satan and his minions. In consequence, they focused upon the activities of witches as clear, unmistakable pieces of evidence that the power of Satan really had been unleashed upon the world. Both confessions used the book of *Job* as their focal, supportive text and indeed the book can serve to illustrate the differences of emphasis between them. Protestants, let us say, if asked to express their peculiar point of view, would draw attention to Job's patience during his time of testing by God, whereas Catholics would prefer to point out the nature of Job's suffering and the variant pains he was called on to endure. It was almost a question of necessary division of emphasis, for if the Protestants took one line, Catholics would naturally be obliged to take another. Hence workers of magic, including all manner of witches, found themselves caught up in a confessional debate about good and evil, whose substance may have been old, but whose details were being argued under very particular circumstances.

Thirdly, although magic had formed part of the general intellectual discourse of Western Europe ever since Graeco-Roman times, it was not until the end of the fifteenth century that European intellectuals – the very class which was engaged in these theological battles – became intimately involved in related speculation, the nature of the created universe. Now, these people (and one is thinking of such names as Johann Trithemius, Francesco Pico della Mirandola, Marsilio Ficino, and Cornelius Agrippa), tended to divide magic into three types: natural, demonic, and deceptive. The last was what we would call conjuring-tricks and stage-illusion. The second was the type we have been discussing; magic which depended for its efficacy on the cooperation of evil spirits. The first, however, encompassed aspects of a multiplicity of disciplines – engineering, physics, chemistry, biology. It explored the hidden ('occult') laws of nature, seeking to discover how they worked and what practical applications, if any, might be made by human beings as a result of those discoveries. Entirely religious in its intention, the study of natural magic wanted to find out a little more about the mind of God, and certain forms of magic known as 'Hermetic' or 'ceremonial' invoked good angels or spirits in charge of parts of the universe (such as planetary angels), in order to acquire just such knowledge. Cornelius Agrippa and John Dee are perhaps the most famous examples of scholars undertaking that form of magic for precisely those ends.

Of course, there was theological danger in this activity. Natural magic might easily slip over into demonic magic, which is why Saint Thomas Aquinas condemned it, and the debate about witchcraft questions whether one could reconcile magic with orthodox Catholicism. Magic and theology were thus linked together at the forefront of intellectual argument during the sixteenth century in a way which had never quite happened before, and therefore, after Protestant dissidence had had a generation to settle down and it had become clear that it was unlikely to be seen off in a hurry, magical operators of all kinds came under sustained attack by both sides of the argument. For they, more than anyone else, seemed to embody those deeply disturbing questions which in various ways were exercising everyone's mind, not simply those of university-trained men but, through the effects of religious change and the practical means of books, pamphlets, sermons, and common conversation, those of the uneducated and socially humble, too.

Nevertheless, if these three factors contributed in the second half of the sixteenth century to the production of an intellectual atmosphere receptive to the intensive prosecution of workers of magic, they do not explain why specific areas embarked on these prosecutions at the particular times they did. Local or regional studies are now needed to help clarify this question and suggest a range of possible answers, and fortunately this is the main direction in which witchcraft studies are going, in parts of Europe, at least. A review such as this, which is meant to be short, cannot hope to do justice to the wealth of information which is being uncovered and presented, but one or two brief sketches may help to indicate some of the ways in which current thinking is moving.

The Jesuit Friedrich Spee (1591-1635) wrote in his book on witchcraft trials, 'Behold Germany, the mother of so many witches [*sagae*]!' It is a vivid apostrophe, easily misunderstood; for one must be quite clear that 'Germany' here is a concept, not the modern geographical area, and refers to a collection of several hundred different states, each guarding its own (though limited) judicial sovereignty under the aegis of the Holy Roman Empire. Each had its own governor – elector, prince, archbishop, or a dozen other titles. Some states were ruled by an ecclesiastic, some by a layperson. By the second half of the century, some were Catholic, others Lutheran or Calvinist. The opportunities for variance in relation to witches and other magical operators were therefore immense, and it is worth bearing in mind that until the Protestant reformations took hold, the Peasant Wars ravaged whole German-speaking regions and the radical Anabaptist movement made inroads into German religious consciousness, there was no great call in any of these areas to prosecute workers of magic in any of its forms. Neither Catholic Tyrol, nor the Calvinist electorate of the High Palatinate, nor the jumble of territories known as Juliers-Cleves-Berg, for example, saw significant numbers of executions, although Juliers seems to have had a problem with werewolves, which it related to the practice of witchcraft.

The most intense pursuits, indeed, seem to have taken place where the ruler was most particularly willing to cooperate with popular demand for them. Thus, the Catholic archbishops of Cologne, Mainz, and Trier presided over a large number of trials and executions during the four decades between c.1580 and c.1620, as did the Catholic bishops of Eichstätt, Bamberg, and Würzburg, while the Lutheran authorities of Schaumburg, Lippe, and Büdingen, and the Calvinist authority of Nassau, although not responsible for as many executions as their Catholic counterparts, still managed to condemn about 2,500 witches between them. It should be emphasized, however, that none of these represents an individual imposing his will upon a reluctant or indifferent populace. Rather, a populace keen to uproot those persons it saw as responsible for crises in its social, economic or religious environment demanded that the authorities pursue the matter through the criminal court and into the burning-ground. The authorities, personally complaisant, therefore obliged.

Why were they happy to do so? Certain rulers, such as the archbishop of Cologne, Frederick of Bavaria, were people of strict piety and were acutely aware of the diabolic forces which menaced the world in which they lived. For some lawyers, witch-trials provided a possible way of advancing their careers, and even where this may not have been the case, the knowledge that their local government favoured the uncovering and execution of witches cannot but have had some effect on their conduct of interrogations and their judgements. As far as pressure from below is concerned, one needs to take into account local as well as general European conditions. In 1625, for example, the Electorate of Cologne saw a concatenation of agricultural problems which produced high prices, famine, and notable mortality, and this may not be unconnected with the large number of prosecutions and executions for witchcraft in that territory. Relevant, too, perhaps, is the weakness or strength of a region's local government. Where it was weak, the populace was able to cast its fears on those it conceived as responsible for causing them and demand of its officials, with some effectiveness, that they do something about the perceived offenders. A universal thesis to explain witch-persecution will therefore not work because outbreaks of prosecutions were local and had local causes.

The same may be noted, broadly speaking, of other European countries, too. Denmark, for example, saw a peak of witchcraft trials before the Jutland County Court during the period

1617–25, a period which coincided with economic problems in the country as a whole. Some Jutland peasants benefited at this time from the high price of grain, others did not, but both groups, not to mention town-dwellers who were likely to be affected by significant movements in prices, cannot have been unaware of the fluctuating economic conditions and seem to have sought to exorcize their fears for the future by pursuing individual workers of magic, about whose malign influence and intention there was common agreement. The local authorities, keen to follow their lead and nervous lest by thwarting it they cause people's charged emotions to turn against officials and government, were happy to oblige and indeed to encourage this popular desire for revenge and liberation.

Another of the triggers of this wave of prosecutions was undoubtedly King Christian IV's hostile decree concerning workers of magic and their accomplices, issued in 1617, but one should note that the judges of the High Court in Jutland were imposing sentences very much lighter than those of the local courts, and thus the point about the importance of our looking at *local* circumstances in relation to witch-trials is made again. It can also be seen if we take into account the views of influential individuals. The Lutheran bishop of Sealand in the 1540s, for example, was Peder Palladius. He was eager to eradicate witches and other magical operators from his diocese, as his visitation book for 1544 makes clear. There he refers to large numbers of them recently burned in Malmø, Køge, and other places, and he urged his flock to denounce such people to the proper authorities. Less than a century later, however, his successor, Jesper Brochmand, was writing that the Devil was unable to produce any real miracles because he had not the power, and that any extraordinary effects attributed to him either rested upon causes not yet understood or were simply illusions. Nor did Brochmand place any credence in the claim of necromancers that they could call up the souls of the dead and enable them to have conversations with the living.[4] Yet it was the more sceptical Brochmand who wielded influence in Sealand at a time when the prosecution rate of witches was at its highest; a circumstance which again tends to suggest that the prosecutions were not led by the Church but by a combination of the laity and the secular authorities.

In some areas the most intense waves of prosecution did not take place until well into the seventeenth century. Sweden, for example, saw its worst outbreak start in the summer of 1668 and continue intermittently until the summer of 1676. These trials are especially notable for their involvement of children as victims and witnesses. Hundreds of them were cited to give evidence that they had been taken magically to Mount Blåkulla where they had witnessed the horrors of the Sabbat, and the sheer quantity of these testimonies proved weighty enough to secure convictions by the local court of eighteen women who were the principal accused in 1668-9. Eleven of the sentences were revoked upon appeal to Stockholm. Nevertheless, a precedent had been set, and the usual safeguards built into Swedish (as into Danish) law to prevent injustice arising from malicious or tainted accusations or the production of evidence from torture were disregarded, largely because the apparent plight and suffering of so many children were involved. Yet again it is clear that the impulse for these initial prosecutions, and for those which followed, came principally from the local population. Indeed, in August 1669, the parish of Mora which was at the centre of the earliest stage, sent a delegation to Stockholm to ask for the implementation of much more stringent official measures to protect their children against the workers of magic. The government hesitated but then did what governments tend to do when faced by intractable problems: it instituted a royal commission. This, however, despite its best efforts, failed to stem the anxiety which quickly turned into a panic and set off further trials, once more fuelled by the evidence of children.

If we now turn from the north of Europe to the south, we encounter countries such as Spain, Portugal, and Italy in which magical practitioners were obliged to face the Holy Office, better known perhaps as 'the Inquisition'. This group of committees (for in spite of modern popular perception, there was more than one Inquisition), developed not only a distinctive attitude towards magical operators but also a particular judicial method of dealing with them. Contrary to the anti-Catholic propaganda of nineteenth- and early-twentieth-century writers on the subject, the Inquisition did not indiscriminately torture innocents and seek to put to death as many of them as possible. In fact, a suspect witch or magician coming before a tribunal of the Inquisition was quite likely to receive a fairer hearing than in many other courts in Europe, and her or his punishment after conviction would almost certainly be lighter. The reason is that the Holy Office instituted and did its best to maintain strict guidelines for the trials of witches (*striges*), diviners (*sortilegii*), and workers of harmful magic (*maleficii*), as a late sixteenth-century directive aimed especially at provincial tribunals of the Inquisition makes clear. The principal interest of the inquisitors when faced by a practiser of magic was simple: do the charges against this person involve heresy or not? If they did not, the inquisitors were more than likely to treat the magical content of the accusations as evidence of the defendant's silliness or ignorance, and dismiss her or him with an explanation of why these magical acts were undesirable, and a warning not to repeat them.

Malta provides an interesting example of southern European experience of magic. Worshipping the Devil – the most obviously heretical act in the range of magical behaviours, and the one most unmistakable in occurrences of the Sabbat – scarcely makes an appearance. The Devil might indeed appear to women in particular, but as individual to individual, often in a sexual context. Betta Caloiro, for example, maintained during her interrogation on 25 June 1601, that she had had an intimate relationship with him since she was twelve. She called him *farfarello* (a nocturnal spirit who plays tricks with people's minds and emotions), and associated him with fairies (*fati*) whom she also saw at night. Similar confessions can be found in Scottish records. Nothing could be further from the pernicious and disturbing diabolism of the Sabbat, and one can therefore see why the Holy Office – unlike the Scottish Kirk, which inter- preted these encounters as evidence of 'standard' demonic witchcraft – was prepared to take a relatively detached view of beliefs and practices which diverged so far from that 'standard' demonological theory.

Maltese magicians, like their counterparts elsewhere in Europe, also attempted to heal the sick by means of various invocations (many of them based on Catholic prayers), or by using the names of those saints who were patrons of the illness in question as Names of Power. One of their most needed skills was countering the evil eye. Helena, the wife of Pietro Periano, claimed to be able to mitigate or heal its effects by washing and fumigating her patient and then reciting 'Our Father', 'Hail Mary', the Creed, and a spell in Maltese which clearly owed nothing to religion but said nothing about demonic assistance either. Such mixtures of Catholic prayers with a magical ceremony were the preferred method of dealing with illness among Maltese (and, indeed, other Mediterranean) women. The reaction of the Church was to condemn these practices and make vigorous efforts to eradicate their use, but the Holy Office did not seek to destroy the people who used or requested them.

In 1617, for example, Sulpitia de Lango was caught in the act of secreting an instrument of love-magic beneath the altar-cloth in the Grand Masters' crypt of the Hospitallers' church in Valletta. She was summoned before the Inquisition to answer for her actions, along with three other people involved in the magical operation. Once the inquisitors were satisfied they had got to the bottom of the incident, they passed sentence, which was that all four should confess and receive communion for four years on specified feast days. Sulpitia, who had already appeared before the Inquisition on two previous occasions on charges of practising magic, and had twice broken her promise to abjure it, was also condemned to be flogged and then imprisoned for eight years. After two of these had passed, however, she appealed successfully against this part of her sentence and was released.

Such reasonable punishment and willing clemency help to illustrate the point that, far from acting as an organ of savage repression, the Inquisition actually acted as a brake upon popular lay demands for greater severity. Indeed, senior inquisitors frequently wrote to provincial tribunals to urge upon them great care in the gathering of evidence, especially *before* imprisoning or torturing a suspect. Hence, it is interesting to find that in the mid-seventeenth century, secular courts were complaining that the Holy Office was far too lax in prosecuting witches, and were seeking to extend their own, far more severe, jurisdiction over such matters.

When it came to the New World – New Spain in Central and South America, New England further north, and New France further north still – the Europeans brought with them preconceptions of what they might discover. Greek, Roman, and then medieval writers may have presented them with a curious gallimaufry of strange lands and strange peoples, misremembered real experiences, or indulged in speculation intended to fill gaps in their knowledge, but by doing so they had prepared explorers, traders, and missionaries for the discovery that Earth contained a multitude of extraordinary sights and wonders. These, of course, required explanation and by natural inclination the visitors turned to current theological and sociological assumptions to provide the answers they sought. These assumptions, however, were often built upon a reading of those same Classical and medieval authors, and referring to a codified past to explain an exotic present was an intellectual habit which persisted as ethnographers wrote their treatises and missionaries their reports long after the first generation of Europeans had witnessed the American continent.

I have not contented myself with knowing the character of the savages and informing myself about their customs and practices [wrote the Jesuit missionary Joseph Lafitau in 1724]. 'I have sought in these practices and customs traces of the most remote antiquity. I have read carefully those of the most ancient authors who have discussed the customs, laws, and usages of peoples about whom they had some knowledge. I have compared these customs (ancient and savage), and I confess that if the ancient authors have given me some insights to support the several happy conjectures regarding the savages, the customs of the savages have given me some insights to understand the ancient authors more easily and to explain several things in their writings.

Moeurs des sauvages Ameriquains 1.3-4

Foremost among the subjects requiring elucidation was religion, and here Europeans were faced by something of a dilemma. They could either view native religious beliefs and practices with unmitigated horror, as did the Spanish historian and theologian, Ginés Sepúlveda, who argued that the idolatrous barbarity of the Amerindians was sufficient reason to make war upon them as a punishment, or seek out those parts which conformed to their notions of 'good', while dismissing others which they interpreted as 'bad'. Lafitau did his best with the latter. On native religion he observed that since knowledge of it 'has come to us only in the period of its corruption, it could only ever have appeared to us as a monstrous religion. Indeed, it is shrouded in all the darkness of idolatry and all the horrors of magic [which are] fruitful sources of the greatest crimes, the most pitiable bewilderment of spirit, and the greatest emotional disorders'. Nevertheless, he added, this corruption is not so general that one cannot find in the religion some principles opposed to corruption, a sentiment which would have been recognized and perhaps applauded by his fellow Jesuit, José de Acosta (1540-1600), who noted, more than a century earlier, that one should not conceive Amerindian history as one long diabolic hallucination but should remember that the Greeks and Romans too practised rites which now seem debased and even criminal.

The New World, then, could easily be interpreted either as a place languishing under the domination of Satan, or as a brave exotic region peopled by noble savages who simply needed to have their rough edges smoothed by contact with Christian Europe. In either case, however, there was much for missionaries to do, and yet even a couple of generations after the advent of Christianity, the new official religion had not eliminated the old, and the two might be found co-existing as distinctly uneasy neighbours. Thus, in 1621, the Jesuit Pablo José de Arriaga lamented the extent to which native Peruvians were given to 'superstition', noting among other examples the way women in childbirth called upon witches (*hechiceros*) to help them by offering sacrifice to the old gods, or the distasteful practice of disinterring the dead from churches and taking them elsewhere, on the grounds that the corpse could not rest easily in a Christian sepulture.[5]

But what was the Church's reaction to these provocations and partial failures? The local Inquisition could be ruthless in eliminating dangerous opponents of the new religious regime. In Mexico, for example, a leading native aristocrat who concealed in his house a painting which the inquisitors deemed demonic was handed over to the secular arm and burned in 1539, while in the following year they did the same to one Martín Ocelotl who was plotting revolution and predicting the end of the world. These, however, were as much political as religious deaths. Similarly, there were those (such as the idolatrous Juan Luis who in 1598 said that he believed the Devil was more powerful than God, or Juan Francisco who in 1608 blasphemously knocked four images off a Catholic altar) who caused the Inquisition to react with vigour as it tried to find out whether or not their actions were signs of a widespread diabolism which might threaten the stability of the Christian faith – a suspicion reminiscent of contemporary European fears that witches could be part of a large conspiracy engineered and controlled by Satan against the Church.

But these defendants were men and their offences not typical of the magic or witchcraft which came before the Mexican Inquisition. Far more common were accusations of love-magic brought against women. The reason for this appears to be a simple transference of Castilian concerns across the Atlantic. For Spanish magic, like magic in the rest of Europe, was not a unified set of beliefs and practices. In northern Spain, magic and witchcraft tended to bear a closer resemblance to their counterparts elsewhere in Europe, whereas in the south witches addressed themselves rather more to controlling men through magical modification of their sexual behaviour. Hence the predominance of amatory spells.

The witchcraft of Mexico was thus very similar to that of southern Spain, not so much on account of any necessary similarity between the two as because this is how the European officials based there interpreted what they saw and what they were told. This can even be seen in their expectation of finding magical practices among certain social groups. In southern Spain, moriscos were frequently seen as healers. In Mexico, preternatural powers were attributed to creoles, half-castes, Hispanicized Indians, and African slaves. (These, at any rate, were the groups subject to inquisitorial discipline, Amerindians being free by decree from control by the Inquisition since it was thought they needed time to adapt to and integrate into the new faith.) The Inquisition therefore reacted to magical operators in the Catholic New World very much as it did to their European counterparts, and for the same reasons. Unlike secular authorities who wanted to establish a person's legal responsibility for the crime of which he or she was accused, the

Inquisition was interested in individual conscience and repentance, and once the former had been unburdened and the latter expressed, the aim of the Inquisition had been achieved.

If we now look north, however, we shall see a rather different situation. Jesuit missionaries among the Huron and Iroquois not only encountered native magic but were themselves sometimes accused of being witches. Both peoples believed that an illness might stem from one of two causes. It could be natural, in which case they would employ natural remedies although, as Lafitau said of the Iroquois, the gathering and preparation of the requisite herbs would be accompanied by 'a number of common superstitions' – in other words, magical sounds and gestures, entirely comparable to similar situations in Europe. On the other hand, the illness might be caused by maleficent magic or witchcraft, in which case the patient or the patient's family would call in a shaman whose task was to detect and thus confirm the preternatural origin of the malady, and then to remove it and thus effect a cure.

According to Huron and Ojibwa belief, the witch had magically inserted the instrument of his or her malefice – almost any kind of small object, such as a tuft of hair or an animal's claw – into the patient's body. Getting rid of this instrument was done by making the patient vomit, by sucking it out of his or her flesh, or by performing a magical or symbolic operation with a knife. In some ways this process is reminiscent of one of the common symptoms of Europeans possessed by an evil spirit, in which the sufferer vomits small objects – pins, stones, hair – both as a sign of possession and as a symptom of relief. Iroquois curers, some of whom were observed in 1634 by the Dutch barber-surgeon, Harmen van den Bogaert, set out to catch the evil spirit responsible for the illness and trample it to death. This they did first by stamping upon bark and reducing it to dust which they blew in each other's direction, then one of their number took hold of an otter, sucked upon the neck and back of the sick person, and spat into the otter's mouth. Unfortunately, Van den Bogaert saw little more of the ceremony because he was frightened and ran away. But he learned enough about Iroquois witchcraft to be able to tell us that witches (who could be men or women), might assume the shapes of animals while practising their malefices and that they were motivated to do harm by envy, a causative impulse also attributed to witches by the Huron. In Europe, by contrast, envy tended to be associated with the evil eye rather than with witch-craft as such, and therefore the person with the evil eye was not necessarily designated a witch.

Both Huron and Iroquois were prepared to kill their witches as a way of putting a stop to the spread of their magical harm. Among the Huron, theoretically anyone who felt threatened by another's magic had the right to kill him or her. But in practice this right was curtailed by allowing the suspect time to respond to threats, modify the behaviour which caused suspicion in the first place, and so reintegrate into society once again. But from time to time this fear of witches exhibited itself either in trials for witchcraft before local chiefs and elders, or in formal denun-ciations by a chief or village council. In both instances a sentence of death was likely to follow a guilty verdict, and in those cases where a defendant had been judged in secret during his or her absence, an executioner was appointed to kill the witch on sight without any warning.

Between 1634 and 1640 the Huron were visited by a series of epidemics. At first, they turned to their traditional ways of coping. Assuming more or less from the start that the outbreaks had been caused by witchcraft, they both made and listened to accusations of maleficent magic, levelled against individuals, some of whom were tortured to make them confess and so nullify the effect of their magic, while others were put to death. But it was also widely accepted among the native peoples that the Jesuit missionaries were the agents behind the sickness. The fact that the Jesuits were celibate, keen to live among the Huron, and frequently sought to counter the power of native shamans by performing religious rituals intended to stem the advance of the epidemics, was taken as a sign that the Fathers were not so much benign priests as active witches. The images in their chapels, the consecrated Hosts they administered at communion, the water they used in baptism, even the food and medicines they distributed to the needy the Huron regarded as no better than instruments of foreign witchcraft. In consequence, the Jesuits came under increasing pressure to retire from Huron territory, and in 1637 and 1640 there was even talk among the Huron chiefs about whether the Jesuit witches should be put to death.

The experience of Catholic Europeans in New Spain and New France thus offers an interesting contrast in reaction. Where the Inquisition was dominant, the Church took control of the lives of the native peoples and from this process emerged a peculiar amalgam of magico-religious beliefs and practices. Witchcraft was treated more or less as it would have been in the Old World – a matter of ignorance and silliness, deserving of reprimand and punishment, to be sure, but not pursued to the death because it was not seen as evidence of a counter-Church erected by Satan in his apocalyptic struggle with God. New France, on the other hand, tended to rely on the work of missionaries without the assistance of an Inquisitional tribunal. The native peoples were therefore not so readily subject to religious domination, there was no amalgamation of religious cultures, and the well-meaning efforts of the Jesuit Fathers to out-magic their opponents after the manner of Moses competing with Pharaoh's magicians either came to nothing or had an effect opposite to the one intended.

In Protestant New England, things were rather different. The sources are rather sparse, but we have enough to tell us that techniques of divining, healing, doing magical harm and protecting oneself against such malefice had crossed the Atlantic and were flourishing in every part of these northern colonies. One of the earliest surviving records, for example, tells us that Margaret Jones, a cunning woman from Massachusetts, could not only heal the sick or delay their recovery, but also foretell the future. When she was arrested on a charge of practising witchcraft, a body search revealed that she had a teat in her pudenda, and witnesses attested they had seen her demon-familiar in the form of a small child which unaccountably vanished when pursued. Margaret was executed in 1648, protesting her innocence to the last, but quite possibly guilty (like so many accused witches) of practising magic in one form or another and at least to some degree.

Church ministers, of course, took a dim, not to say severe view of these activities and would not even allow their congregations the defence of counter-magic by way of personal protection. Their argument was the standard Protestant adjuration. God was testing the individual's spiritual fortitude and punishing his or her sins. The only proper defence against magical attack, therefore, was to acknowledge one's failings and turn to God in faith.

Prayer [observed the minister Deodat Lawson] is the most proper and potent antidote against the old Serpent's venomous operations.

When legions of devils do come down among us, multitudes of prayers should go up to God. Satan, the worst of all our enemies, is called in Scripture a dragon, to note his malice; a serpent, to note his subtlety; a lion, to note his strength. But none of all these can stand before prayer.

Christ's Fidelity, 1692

New England, however, was not a uniform religious society. Not everyone was a Puritan – Goodwife Glover from Boston, for example, was a Catholic and used counter-magic in the form of rag dolls – and not every Puritan was devout. Ministers' exhortations therefore might well fail to have the desired effect on everyone. But actually the very form of religion preached by those same ministers can be seen as a contributory cause of insecurity and uneasiness among those who listened to them. When the Puritan preacher, Cotton Mather, delivered 'An Hortatory and Necessary Address to a Country now Extraordinarily Alarum'd by the Wrath of the Devil', what range of responses was his discourse likely to produce from his congregation? He constantly repeated his text, 'the Devil is come down unto us with great wrath', and issued warnings and exhortations which the modern reader might think were almost designed to engender extreme anxiety in his listeners:

In many ways, for many years hath the Devil been assaying to Extirpate the Kingdom of our Lord Jesus here... Devils have obtain'd the power, to take on them the likeness of harmless people, and in that likeness to afflict other people... Let the Devils *coming down in great wrath upon us*, cause us to *come down* in *great grief* before the Lord... How much more now ought we to *humble ourselves* under that *Mighty Hand* of that God who indeed has the *Devil* in a *chain*, but has horribly lengthened out the *Chain!*... 'Tis to be feared, the Children of *New-England* have *secretly* done many things that have been pleasing to the Devil. They say, that in some Towns it has been a usual thing for People to cure Hurts with *Spells*, or to use detestable Conjurations, with *Sieves, Keys*, and *Pease*, and *Nails*, and *Horse-shoes*, and I know not what other Implements, to learn the things for which they have a forbidden, and an impious *Curiosity*. 'Tis in the Devil's Name, that such things are done; and in God's Name I do this day charge them, as vile Impieties... The Devil is a Prince, yea, the Devil is a God unto all the Unregenerate; and alas, there is *A Whole World of them*. Desolate Sinners, consider what an horrid Lord it is that you are Enslav'd unto.

*The Wonders of the Invisible Worl*d, 1692

It would be no surprise, then, if a siege mentality developed in New England. The people, as they made clear by their frequent resorting to various forms of magic, were concerned with countering their fears and seeking efficient protection against assaults from the ever-present powers of darkness, and we must recollect that they also had all too many material anxieties which added to their unease: threat of attacks from Indians, political struggles of their own, and, if they were newly-arrived from the Old World, the natural worries about their success or failure in their new environment. Ministers, for their part, were keen to stamp out any manifestations of magical beliefs and practices, and yet their open hostility to operations which their flocks saw as mechanisms of defence, sources of comfort, alleviations of their unease, and spy-glass into an uncertain future, merely served to heighten the tension and make people feel they were increasingly helpless just at a time when Satan was advancing his troops upon their community.

The Salem witchcraft trials of 1692 in Massachusetts, which so dominate discussion of witchcraft in North America (largely because their records are unusually full), actually furnish quite a good example of the way inner tensions could burst into the open and threaten a local society. These tensions were various. Two families, the Putnams and Porters, had been at odds for several years before the alleged witchcraft surfaced, and of course each family had its supporters and its opponents. The Porters were beginning to enjoy a certain amount of economic success, and the Putnams interpreted this in terms of their own relative decline. Hence grew factionalism. Then a new minister, Samuel Parrish, arrived in Salem. Samuel's father had been a merchant in Barbados and at first his son followed him in that trade. But in the mid-1680s he had decided to enter the ministry, and by the end of the decade he settled down in Salem, largely at the invitation of the Putnams who approved of his particular brand of Puritanism.

Parrish brought with him a slave, Tituba, who was well-acquainted with Caribbean magic from her days in Barbados and was therefore able, should the need arise, to provide counter-magic for those who requested it. Her help was soon needed. Parrish's daughter Elizabeth, aged nine, and her cousin Abigail Williams, aged eleven, started to exhibit, most dramatically, the symptoms of people possessed by evil spirits. They were followed by others, and all began to accuse members of their community of being responsible for their condition. The local doctor and the ministers concurred that these increasingly frightening episodes were caused by witchcraft, and it was not long before a remarkable number of persons was accused of bewitching the children and adolescents concerned. Not everyone found him or herself in court, but there were sufficient defendants to make the trials a sensation.

Those in the dock answered the charges, often in the face of histrionic fits and shriekings from their accusers, as best they could, according to their individual fears and abilities. Susanna Martin, for example, who was tried on 29 June 1692 showed herself undaunted by her judicial ordeal. One charge dealt with the effects of her evil eye. At her first examination before the magistrates, her accusers had reacted to her looking at them by flinging themselves upon the floor, as though struck by the evil eye. Cotton Mather records the following exchange between Susanna and the Magistrate.

Magistrate: Pray, what ails these People?

Martin: I don't know.

Magistrate: But what do you think ails them?

Martin: I don't desire to spend my Judgment upon it.

Magistrate: Don't you think they are bewitch'd?

Martin: No, I do not think they are.

Magistrate: Tell us your Thoughts about them then.

Martin: No, my thoughts are my own, when they are in, but when they are out they are anothers. Their Master——

Magistrate: Their Master? who do you think is their Master?

Martin: If they be dealing in the Black Art, you may know as well as I.

Magistrate: Well, what have you done towards this?

Martin: Nothing at all.

Magistrate: Why, 'tis you or your Appearance.

Martin: I cannot help it.

Magistrate: Is it not *your* Master? How comes your Appearance to hurt these?

Martin: How do I know?

It is interesting to see Susanna doing her best to evade the forensic attempt to get her to incriminate herself, even to the point of suggesting that her accusers themselves may be actively engaged in magic, but her resistance proved vain and she was found guilty as charged and hanged on 19 July.

The Salem trials catch one's attention because they exhibit, in more detail than is often available elsewhere, many of the features familiar to us from witch trials in Europe: alleged possession of pre-pubertal children and young adults, the devastating effect of children's evidence when accepted by credulous adults (examples of which we have had in recent times in investigations into alleged Satanic abuse of children), the growth of panic in a community already filled with familial and neighbourhood tensions, and the dislocation of comprehensions between officials and those whose behaviour they were seeking to regulate. The core of the Salem trials, in fact, has nothing specifically American about it, and the sight of a nerve-wracked community, tearing at itself in an effort to alleviate tensions which had become unbearable, could have been witnessed almost anywhere in Europe where the requisite degree of local stress existed. Unlike New Spain or New France where the interaction between European immigrants and local native peoples affected both parties' perceptions of magical behaviour, Salem seems to have behaved (perhaps not unsurprisingly), rather like an English parish, looking inward rather than outward for both the causes and the solutions to its self-engendered panic.

CHAPTER FOUR

Trying a Witch

I t is only with fairly recent scholarship that we are beginning to have a somewhat clearer understanding of who was likely to be accused of witchcraft. Our sources are many and various, and available space allows me to deal with only one or two of them, but they have to be treated with considerable care – something which has not always been done in the past and is not always done in the present when sensationalism triumphs over historical probability.

Court records, for example, vary considerably in their detail. Some may be highly abridged résumés of a process, consisting of the accused person's name, a general indication of the charge or charges against her or him, and perhaps a note of the verdict and sentence, although it should be emphasized that in very many, perhaps a majority, of cases we do not know whether the defendant was found guilty or innocent. The rate of 'not guilty' verdicts could be high – in the High Court of Justiciary in Scotland, for example, it has been reckoned at fifty per cent – and it is usually impossible for us to know whether in the case of multiple charges against an individual the accused was found guilty (or indeed innocent) of every one or only some of them. Various legal systems were in operation in Western Europe and the Americas, too. It would have been a very different matter for the accused to appear before a single judge or panel of judges who were responsible for assessing the evidence, coming to a verdict and passing sentence, or to stand trial in a court which had a jury to adjudge guilt or innocence, and which allowed or provided a counsel for the defence.

The quality of the judge was also important, and the Polish Bishop Casimir Czartorinski was just one who complained bitterly, in 1669, that the strict rules for examination of suspect witches, use of torture, and conduct of their trial were all too often ignored or flouted by ignorant, brutish officials. What was recorded, therefore, depended in part on what was done, who was doing it, and indeed on the circumstances in which the interrogation or trial was taking place. Was it an isolated instance of alleged witchcraft, or one of an interconnected series? Was the court sitting in the middle of a witch-panic, and did the judge or judges have the standing or courage to disagree with popular clamour to find the accused guilty and have her executed forthwith? Was the court made up of ecclesiastics or laymen or a mixture of the two? The circumambient atmosphere of the examination and the trial cannot but have affected all those concerned, including those whose job it was to set down what was said and done.

We also have to bear in mind the qualifications and abilities of the notary and the conventions by which he recorded the proceedings. Most seem to have heeded (consciously or not), the words of the fourteenth-century inquisitor, Bernardo Gui, that notaries should transcribe only those words which concern the substance of the matter in hand and which seem best to express the truth (*Practica inquisitionis heretice pravitatis*). A censoring procedure was thus at work, with the result that the final document tells us what the clerk thought it appropriate for us to know, not from any sinister motive of concealment but simply out of convention and the understandable need to abbreviate. The notaries themselves, by definition more learned than many of the defendants whose interrogations and trials they were committing in some form to paper, may have been required by law, or again by convention, to record the proceedings in Latin. This meant that they were translating from the vernacular, and indeed if the defendant answered questions in his or her local dialect, the answers may well have needed to be translated first into a vernacular readily understood by the court before the notary translated an abbreviated version of that vernacular version into Latin. When we read the surviving result, therefore, we may be considerably removed from the original wording of the principals in the case.

It is also necessary to ask what it was the court officials were trying to record. The judge had his agenda, so did the defendant. By the time written evidence was ready to be produced in court and witnesses were ready to give their testimonies, a great deal of work had already been done to reduce narratives to their essentials and make (or at least try to make) them conform to the court's expectations. This could mean that if, let us say, a defendant gave an account of meeting fairies – a common feature of many witch confessions in certain places – the interrogators or judges might prefer to regard these 'fairies' as 'evil spirits', since this would not only fit standard early-modern witchcraft theory, but would also simplify the charges to be considered. Under pressure, the defendant might agree to the re-interpretation or might choose to stand by his or her version of events. What we read in court records is thus a number of interlocking narratives which have been shaped beforehand in circumstances about which we may know little or nothing, and subsequently modified in a number of different ways for different reasons. We must not, therefore, treat these documents as though they were verbal photographs of an event, unposed, untampered with, realistic in every detail. They are, rather, sketches of abbreviations of one précis after another, not always conveying their information in the original tongues of the participants.

Witchcraft treatises were written by learned men for the instruction and use of other learned men. They were attempts to describe and define a series of theological problems. What is the extent of Satan's power within the created universe? Why does God allow him latitude? What makes certain people reject God and adhere to Satan? What is the range of activities permitted to these people, and where do their boundaries lie? What is the relationship between natural and demonic magic? How far can the apparent effects of magic be attributed to human trickery, demonic illusion, or physical or mental illness? Is it permissible to use magic to counter unwanted or harmful magic? How can magical operations best be resisted by society, and what are the legal means whereby society can protect itself against them? Deeply serious questions, treated seriously by everyone.

Now, each treatise, as one might expect, bears the stamp of the man who wrote it. Martín del Rio (1551-1608) was a Jesuit and a Classical scholar, who produced one of the most comprehensive and influential works on magic after becoming interested in the case of a Benedictine monk, Jean del Vaulx, who was tried for witchcraft in 1597. *Disquisitiones Magicae* (Investigations into Magic), published in 1599-1600, covers every aspect of the subject and, contrary to what is often written about its author, evinces a degree of scepticism or at least reservation on several points of witchcraft, such the reality of the witch's mark or the usefulness of the swimming test. Encyclopaedic in his reading, meticulous in his argumentation, Del Rio presents his audience with a massive treatise intended to show, with finality, how wrong, how dangerous, and how subtle all forms of magic are. But, by linking magic firmly to heresy, he produced a work which was also meant to be a major weapon for Catholic apologists in their theological war with Protestants; one needs to keep this in mind while reading the book and to note how Del Rio structures his commentary upon magic and its operators.

Writers upon magic were not, however, all theologians. Four French lawyers, Jean Bodin (1529-1596), Nicolas Rémy (c.1530-1612), Pierre de Lancre (1553-1631), and Henri Boguet (c.1550-1619), all wrote from personal experience of witch trials and were all convinced that witches presented such a grave threat to the stability of society that they needed to be extirpated as efficiently and as ruthlessly as possible. Bodin, a political philosopher of great repute as well as a lawyer, emphasized this point especially. His treatise, written in French rather than in Latin, *De la démonomanie des sorciers* (The Demon-Insanity of Sorcerers), also underlined the difficulty of which everyone was aware – the problem of proving a charge of witchcraft by the standards of proof required in other capital offences – and suggested strongly that therefore the usual legal safeguards ought to be waived in this case. The evidence of children, for example, should be heard and noted. Peter Binsfeld (c.1540-1603), Catholic bishop of Trier, was equally keen to encourage wide-scale prosecution. His book, *Tractatus de confessionibus maleficorum et sagarum* (Treatise on the Confessions of Workers of Harmful Magic and Witches), appeared in 1589 as a result of his particular interest in the trial of one Dietrich Flade, a prominent layman in Trier (Vice-

Governor of the city, Rector of the university), who was charged as a witch during a purge throughout the 1580s of heretics, Jews, and magical workers by the bishop of Trier, Johann von Schönenburg.

Personal experience of witch trials also stimulated the Jesuit Friedrich von Spee (1591-1635) to produce his *Cautio Criminalis* (Precautions to be Taken in Criminal Trials) in 1631. Horrified by the way in which he saw evidence being obtained, he issued what was in effect an impassioned plea for the restoration of justice and, like the Protestant physician Johann Wier (1515-1588), provided vivid examples of the way in which the provisions of the German legal system were being abused. Wier wrote two books on witches. In *De praestigiis daemonum et incantationibus ac veneficiis* (The Deceptive Tricks of Evil Spirits, Incantations, and Works of Poisonous Magic), published in 1563, he suggested that many witches might actually be suffering from an imbalance of their humours with a predominance of black bile which would result in pronounced melancholia.[1] This was not an idea original to Wier, however. In the chapter to which I have just referred, he quotes extensively from an earlier Italian polymath, Girolamo Cardano, and the interpretation of some witchcraft claims as delusion or insanity can actually be found in several other medical and legal works of the period. It formed, in fact, one of the major debates between writers on magic and witchcraft.

To these two principal and most commonly used sources of information, one should add sermons (some of them preached at the execution site itself), chronicles, travellers' accounts of their experiences, poems, popular pamphlets, personal letters and, of course, pictures. Again, each one of these has an agenda and should not be treated as though it were an indifferent account of the persons or events it describes. When the *Brevísima relación de la destrución de las Indias*, by a Catholic writer, Bartolomé de las Casas, appeared in English translations, his compassionate and emotive description of Amerindian sufferings at the hands of European colonisers was turned into anti-Catholic propaganda by the simple device of changing its title – *Popery Truly Display'd in its Bloody Colours* – a reminder that literature during the sixteenth and seventeenth centuries was always liable to serve or be made to serve religious or political purposes beyond the declared intention of the individual work. Witchcraft material is no different and furnishes a minefield for the unwary or careless reader.

Pictures provide their own interesting problems. It has frequently been the habit to illustrate books on witchcraft with pictures drawn from a number of different places and periods without discrimination – one of Goya's pictures of witches appearing beside a text discussing sixteenth-century Germany, to take a case in point, is as inappropriate as using Constable's *Hay Wain* in a chapter on medieval French farming methods. Pictures are, in fact, as difficult to interpret as text. Plate 12, for example, shows the various stages of a witch's preparing to fly to a Sabbat. She makes her magical unguent, anoints herself, and then flies up her chimney astride a broomstick. The picture comes from a book by Thomas Erastus, *Deux dialogues touchant le pouvoir des sorcières et de la punition qu'elles méritent* (Two Dialogues on the Power of Witches, and on the Punishment They Deserve). Now, it is important to know that Erastus was a physician and a Zwinglian theologian; that he was a German; that his book was published in 1570, well before any serious widespread outbreak of witch prosecutions in the southern German states; that he strongly disapproved of the tempered scepticism of his fellow German physician, Johann Wier; that he believed witches could do nothing themselves but relied entirely upon Satan to produce their magical effects; and that he was of the opinion that those who consulted magical practitioners were as condemnable as the practitioners themselves. All these points affect the way the reader looks at the illustration.

But there are other questions which require answers before we are able to use rather than just view the picture. Who engraved it, the author or someone else? If it is the work of someone else, did the two men consult one another? Did the illustrator read the book in advance, or are we looking at a picture altogether divorced from its accompanying text? Does the picture illustrate popular local belief or learned demonological theory, or is it a fancy based on the illustrator's personal convictions? Was the illustrator a Catholic or a Protestant? Why has he included a man peeping in through a crack in the door? Is this man symbolic of the reader, or does he refer the reader to a particular story about a particular witch? Not every book about witches was illustrated, so when we come across such pictures we must not allow ourselves the luxury or the idleness of a quick glance before returning to concentrate on the words alone. The author included pictures for a purpose, and even asking simple questions about them helps to alert us to the wider implications of pictorial messages which might otherwise pass us by.

It is today, and to an extent it was in the medieval and early modern periods, a cliché that the female witch was old, ugly, and poor. As far as illustrations are concerned, this cliché will not hold up. To be sure, such pictures are common enough, but their context is very important. Woodcuts illustrating popular pamphlets, for example, can be relied on to produce this crude shorthand. It is similar to modern tabloids on homosexuals –

every gay man is limp-wristed, effeminate, and dresses in women's clothes whenever possible – even though the wider, or personal experience of the tabloids' readers will tell them this is nonsense. Still, even these popular illustrations do not always conform to the tabloid pattern. They may, for example, depict witches as young or middle-aged women dressed in accordance with their station in life, and we must ask ourselves, is this meant to convey the subliminal message that witches need not be old or marginal figures, and that they can come from any walk of life? If so, the message would reflect something the reader knew perfectly well from experience. His or her local witch or cunning person could well be a neighbour, someone who looked just like him or her.

But young, beautiful, female witches also formed part of the formal culture of painting, independent of printed texts. In 1523, for example, Hans Baldung Grien (c.1484-1545) painted two witches summoning bad weather, *Die Wetterhexen*. Both are self-consciously posed with a sensual elegance to tempt the viewer's immediate attention. The seated witch seems to be doing the actual work of raising a storm, with the help of a demon-child, while the other looks back seductively at us, covering the nakedness we *cannot* see with a sheet which rises, penis-like, from the half-concealed demon-goat revealed by the casual sideways slouch of her leg. She reminds us of Eve or Venus, a visualization of the one of the messages of the *Malleus Maleficarum* – female witches trap men into sin by appealing to their lust. Baldung Grien, however, was not a Catholic, but a fervent supporter of Luther, and had received his painterly training from Dürer, inheriting, to some extent, Dürer's sense of the witch as a figure of immense power and energy and sexual disorder. Dürer, in his turn, is likely to have been influenced by the woodcuts illustrating Ulrich Molitor's witchcraft treatise of 1489. So there is an inheritance of attitude towards the visual treatment of witches to be considered, whether the individual painter continues it or consciously develops it in a different direction. If he does the former, does this tell us that the popular or courtly beliefs of his intended audience had not changed very much over the years? If the latter, may we infer change and if so, what kind of change?

Baldung Grien's Italian contemporary, Dosso Dossi (c. 1486–1542), served as court painter to two successive dukes of Ferrara. His picture of the Classical 'witch' Circe [plate 15], painted in 1511–12, also depicts a posed, naked woman, young and beautiful. But the effect is entirely different from that offered by Grien's weather-witches. At first glance, Circe seems to be placid, calm, in an almost frozen landscape which compares strikingly with the background Grien has given his witches – a menacing, dissonant sulphur yellow sky shading uneasily to orange. Certainly Dossi's witch is also a woman in control of her environment. The animals which surround her were originally men, her lovers whom her magic has transformed into creatures either obedient to humans (the dogs) or hunted by them (the stag and the deer), and the two birds perched above her, left and right, are both birds of prey. Circe's calm authority is therefore not alluring but chilling, her naked beauty not so much sensual as dangerously unobtainable. The messages Grien and Dossi include in their paintings seemed to be aimed at men. How would their female viewers have received their intentions? It is a question which should be asked of the literature as well, of course, particularly that in the form of popular pamphlets, ballads, and sermons which, unlike learned demonological treatises, were aimed at an audience of both sexes.

We may also learn from a series of illustrations as opposed to a single picture. The woodcuts which appear in Francesco Guazzo's *Compendium Maleficarum* (A Collection of Concise Details about Women Who Work Harmful Magic), published in 1608, are frequently used to illustrate modern books about witchcraft, but give entirely the wrong impression if they are looked at individually. The treatise itself is unexceptional – it was reprinted only once – a standard gallimaufry of quotations from earlier authorities, anecdotal evidence, and recommendations for dealing with the menace witchcraft posed to society. It is assumed throughout that witches will normally be women. If one looks carefully at the accompanying pictures, however, one notices that the majority of them either show a man as the principal actor, or a mixed company of men and women engaging in nefarious magical activities. It is a man, for example, who receives baptism from Satan, a man who receives Satan's mark, and men who dig up a corpse prior to dismembering it to provide instruments for maleficent magic [plate 16]; and both sexes offer their child to Satan, dance with evil spirits, and roast a child over a fire before their cannibal feast [plate 17]. Guazzo's woodcuts therefore may seem to be at variance with official expectation about the gender of witches, but in fact they illustrate the reality of gender balance as it appears in most of the court records. Witchcraft in real life, as opposed to learned theory, involved men in far greater numbers than is popularly imagined.

⊙══✦══⊙

But what actually happened to someone accused of witchcraft? What was the process through which she or he passed from initial accusation to final condemnation or acquittal? To judge from modern popular accounts, it seems to be the assumption that accused witches all underwent more or less the same judicial experience, but a moment's reflection will suggest that this cannot have been so. Different legal jurisdictions, operating under a variety of codes or variations upon a code, at different periods must mean that a fifteenth-century Italian witch's experience will not have been the same as that of a seventeenth-century Swede. Not even the charges levelled against the accused were necessarily much of a muchness. The Portuguese Inquisition, for example, was particularly interested in *saludadores*, healers who claimed to effect their cures by magic. Demonic transvection and attendance at the Sabbat featured strongly in cases heard before courts in south-western Germany. In France there was a rash of cases of possession during the seventeenth century, an obsession which transferred itself to Quebec.

Judicial procedure also varied considerably. In seventeenth-century England, witchcraft cases were often heard before assizes presided over by judges with long training and experience in the law. Judges did not hear cases in the place of their principal residence. Torture was not employed (except upon uncooperative Catholic priests), to elicit a confession. Accused and accusers faced one another in the court-room and exchanged versions of their respective testimonies, and since there were no advocates for the defence or prosecution the role of the judge in controlling court-proceedings was pre-eminent. There was, however, a jury and when all the evidence had been heard to the judge's satisfaction, the jury was asked to bring in a verdict, which it tended to do almost immediately without retiring from the room.

This legal method, however, was peculiar to England and therefore does not provide a very useful exemplar if we wish to gain even a general notion of what went on elsewhere. Proceedings before an Inquisitional tribunal are equally unrepresentative, and ecclesiastical courts had their own rules for conducting cases. The principles of Roman law inherited via the Emperor Justinian's monumental *Code* were the governing principles for the majority of the courts in Western Europe. These required collection of evidence from the accused and witnesses and the submission of this accumulated evidence to the court before the trial began, and it was the task of the investigators to make sure that all relevant points had been covered, so that the trial itself was, in effect, a public drama conducted according to a script already written. In the case of witchcraft, as we have seen before, evidence which *proved* that a crime had been committed was particularly difficult to obtain. The surest proof was a confession by the accused, and Roman law permitted the use of torture as a means of having that confession, along with its attendant evidence and testimony, confirmed. So once again, the role of the judge or judges was extremely important. Their principal task was not to supervise an altercation between the accused and the injured party (although such an altercation might take place at an earlier stage of the legal proceedings), but to sift the written evidence and check that everyone had observed the rules and applied the appropriate safeguards against malicious prosecution, lying, or confessing merely to avoid the continuance or renewal of torture.

Now, such courts may not have had a jury but they often provided some kind of defence for the accused. When Françoise Bonvin stood trial in 1467 on charges of heresy, attending a Sabbat and making snow fall in July to the detriment of a neighbour's vineyard, she had a professional advocate to plead on her behalf before the presiding bishop, and he must have been persuasive, because Françoise was declared innocent and set at liberty. Scotland – a strictly Calvinist country after its reformation – employed a modified system of Roman law and procedure in her courts, and therefore Scottish witch trials can furnish us with a model with many points in common with similar trials elsewhere in Europe. For this reason, I am going to describe an actual case, hitherto unpublished, taken from the archives of the High Court of Justiciary in Edinburgh. It concerns a woman, Janet Cock from Dalkeith, a small town six miles south-east of Edinburgh, who underwent two trials for witchcraft in the autumn and winter of 1661. Now, the two years 1661 and 1662 saw the largest number of prosecutions for witch-craft in Scotland's history. Janet was therefore caught up in the nearest Scotland ever came to a persecution reminiscent of those in southern Germany.

Prior to her trial – and here I suggest details based upon a large number of other Scottish cases from the same period, whose preliminaries have been in some measure preserved – Janet would have been summoned to answer complaints or accusations handed in to her local kirk session (a weekly meeting of the minister and elders of her church). They would have listened to the complaints, which had to be given under oath, heard Janet's explanations and, over a period perhaps lasting several weeks, decided whether the whole business was a matter for local church discipline, or whether it was serious enough to warrant their having Janet arrested and placed in custody. The ministers and elders will have known both Janet and her accusers well. Most accused witches had been accumu-lating a reputation for practising magic, beneficent, malevolent, or both, for quite a long period – ten, twenty, sometimes thirty years – before accusations had reached this stage, so Janet's minister and elders would have been in a good position to judge the merits of the case against her.

Having decided upon the need for a prosecution, the minister would apply to the High Court in Edinburgh and the matter was then taken out of his hands. Advocates would ask for the written evidence which had already been taken, witnesses would be summoned and their testimony recorded, Janet would be examined and her replies set down. If necessary, she would have been confronted by one or more of her hostile witnesses and the results of that confrontation would be added to the growing dossier. Summonses would then be sent out to named men (drawn from a long list of those liable for jury service), and a date and place set for the trial.

Thus it was that on the afternoon of 10 September 1661, Janet Cock appeared before a judge in the session-house in Edinburgh. She was not left to fend for herself. Scotland had always made provision for the accused (in Scotland called the 'panel') to have someone speak in his or her defence. By the end of the sixteenth century this person (the 'proloquitor for the panel') was always a professional advocate provided without regard for the panel's offence or social status, so Janet was at last able to face the judge and jury (the 'assize') in the knowledge that at least one person in the room was there to see to her interests.

There were ten items on her indictment ('dittay'), and it is worthwhile listing them briefly so that we can see the range of offences of which she was accused. The first relates to an incident which had taken place in 1637, about twenty-four years previously. Janet was in the house of Janet Graham, who was burned for witchcraft not long before Janet Cock's own trial. Janet Graham's child was sick and it appears that Janet Cock had probably been called in to work some kind of magical cure. While she was there, Agnes Spindie visited, bringing with her her own child who was in good health at the time. But after leaving Janet Graham's house, Agnes Spindie's child fell sick and later died, while Janet Graham's child recovered, and Janet Cock was accused of magically transferring the sickness from one child to the other.

Now, it is clear that Janet Cock and Agnes Spindie were frequently at loggerheads. On 22 June 1645 both of them were hauled in front of the kirk session in Dalkeith for being drunk, quarrelling violently, and calling each other 'witch', and the session considered the incident serious enough to refer both women to the civil magistrate. What happened there we do not know, but the incident figures as the second item on Janet Cock's dittay. As it is described there, both women were drunk and Janet threatened Agnes with violence, a threat she carried out a week later when, during a second contretemps, she smacked Agnes on the face. Agnes, who was very much the worse for drink, passed out and had to be taken to bed. The minister at the time, Hugh Campbell, came and reproved Janet for her behaviour, but no sooner did he get home than he fell ill of a kind of frenzy and no one could get hold of him for long enough to put him to bed. Meanwhile Agnes's sister came to Janet and asked her to come and make Agnes well again, only to be told by Janet that Agnes was merely drunk and would soon be better. Both the minister's fit and Agnes's passing out were blamed on Janet's practising witchcraft against them, and all three appeared in court as witnesses against her.

While Agnes lay drunk in bed, a young woman who was keeping her company was also seized with a similar incapacity, at which her father, Thomas Aitkin, lost his temper completely and swore he would cut Janet Cock in pieces unless she lifted the magic she had clearly inflicted upon his daughter. The young woman, we are told, made a full recovery. The Aitkin family, however, continued to bear a grudge against Janet Cock, for a James Aitkin accused her of making his daughter take a fit of vomiting one day as she was coming home from school. His wife testified that her daughter was indeed unwell as he described, but unlike her husband she did not attribute the illness to Janet Cock, and when the daughter gave evidence, we learn that the incident must have taken place some years before because at the time of the trial Janet Aitkin was twenty-two and remembered nothing save the fact that she had been ill when she was a child.

Already it is evident that Janet Cock had acquired the reputation in Dalkeith of being a witch, or at least of being someone who was able to practise both curative and maleficent magic. For example, John Richardson and Janet Cock quarrelled because he called her a witch. Not long after, James fell ill and began to blame Janet as the cause of his sickness. Therefore his brother, Thomas, sent for Janet to remove the enchantment from him and thus cure him of his illness. Janet came, but her efforts came to nothing, for James died that same night. Similarly, when James Douglas fell off his horse and suffered injuries from which it seems he later died, he blamed Janet Cock – 'laid his death upon her' is the phrase usually used in these circumstances – as was testified by his servant, Archibald Simpson, who added that his master often said Janet could take the sickness from him. Interestingly enough, however, although James Douglas's wife witnessed to the fact that Janet and her husband had had a falling-out and that James was frightened of Janet, she maintained she had never heard Janet actually threaten James.

But Janet had the misfortune to quarrel with two men called William Scott. One was the man who had arrested her in August, the baillie of Dalkeith; the other was a man of some substance in the town and, judging by his surname, some kind of familial connection, but the records make it clear that he and the baillie were not in fact the same person. Now, it happened that five or six years before Janet's arrest, this second William Scott stabled his horse one night and when the grooms came next morning to open the stable door, the horse leaped out and proved uncontrollable. Whereupon someone advised William Scott to use magical means to discover whether or not his horse had been bewitched. Scott agreed and had one of the horse's shoes removed and heated red hot, the notion being that if maleficent magic had indeed been employed against the horse, the witch would be forced to appear because of a severe pain, magically transferred to her from the heated horse-shoe; and sure enough, Janet Cock turned up at the house for no apparent good reason.

This item on Janet's dittay is interesting, as it reminds us that during the early modern period magic was a universal practice and not one confined simply to a few individuals or small groups of people. Indeed, the likelihood is that members of the assize at Janet's trial may have used such magical means at some time or another, or at the very least accepted such means as a universally known and practised method of solving certain problems.

The fall-out with William Scott may also have precipitated another charge against her. According to Elspeth Pringle, William Scott's wife – Scottish women kept their own names after marriage – while she was lying in bed soon after the birth of her child, Janet and a number of other women came into the room, along with a black man (that is, either a man with a black skin or a man dressed in black), and tried to take the child from her, and when she called upon God for assistance they all suddenly left through the window which was closed at the time.

Other points in Janet's dittay, however, do not so clearly hang upon her having annoyed or quarrelled with someone else. James Wilson testified that as he and two others were bringing back Christian (Christine) Wilson from Niddry to stand trial for witchcraft, a sudden gale blew up and swept Christian into a burn. This James interpreted as a magical attempt by Janet Cock to rescue a fellow witch, although one of his companions on that day, James Blackie, said that there was nothing unusual about the wind and that Christian could equally well have slipped as been swept away. It is not the first time in this trial that a witness for the prosecution casts doubt on the extent of Janet's involvement in the act of which she stands accused, and is one indication among several that many people were doing their best to tell and to judge the truth. Despite the trial's taking place at a time of increasing persecution of witches in Scotland, there is no evidence of prejudice, blood-lust, or hysteria, and the participants could just as well be involved in a trial for theft, or perjury, or arson.

Finally, the court heard that, according to William Calderwood, the minister, and William Scott, the baillie, Janet had been delated (accused) as a witch by various other condemned witches and that she had actually sent for Calderwood and confessed of her own free will to being a witch, and to having given herself to the Devil and to having received his mark in return for the power to avenge herself on Jean Douglas and her daughters who had called her a witch. This confession, the minister and the other witnesses insisted, was obtained without any torture or other pressure at all.

Janet's defence advocate, the proloquitor for the panel, poured scorn on these various charges. A man could fall off his horse and die without the presence of witchcraft. Women in childbed may well be subjected to fevered illusions. Horses become frightened, and buck and kick by nature. People die of natural causes as well as by witchcraft. Was there a sudden gale? Janet is not specifically accused of raising it. As for her confession, she denies it. Here we see the two lines taken by the defence: (a) natural rather than preternatural explanation for events, and (b) legal quibbles about the wording of the dittay. They are more or less the same as those taken by the defence in the trial of Françoise Bonvin nearly two hundred years previously.

The assize, consisting largely of Edinburgh merchants and working men from Dalkeith, retired and considered the evidence. If one reads through the judicial reports of Scottish trials for witchcraft, and through such of their pre-trial papers as survive, perhaps the most intriguing moment comes at that point where one reads the verdict of the assize. Unless it has been given away at the beginning of the account by a marginal note saying 'convict and burnt' or 'clengit' (acquitted) or 'assoiled' (acquitted), it is impossible to guess either from a list of the charges brought against the panel, or from the arguments advanced in her or his favour by the proloquitor whether the assize will find the panel guilty or not. Since there is scarcely ever an opportunity to go behind the scenes, as it were, and listen to deliberations which took place in the assize house, it is usually impossible to know whether the final verdict was unanimous or divided, and whether it was unanimous or divided upon every point of the dittay or only upon some. Occasionally a marginal note will tell us 'una voce' (unanimously) or 'by plurality of voices', but even that is a comment upon the verdict as a whole and not upon individual items of the dittay.

But in Janet's case we know much more than this because the record of the assize's voting has survived (see table on next page). There were ten articles in the dittay and fifteen assizers, fifteen being the usual number for a Scottish assize during this period. The letter 'c' stands for 'clengit' and 'ff' for 'fylit' (guilty).

Upon retiring from the court-room, the assize chose its chancellor (foreman of the jury) and then set to consider what it had heard. After due deliberation, it returned to the court-room and delivered its verdict, though in what form we are unsure. The preservation of the voting in this case indicates that a record of some kind was kept and filed with the papers of the trial, but Janet may not have been given the details, only the blanket decision that she had been acquitted on this occasion. The system worked by totting up the number of 'guilty' and 'innocent' votes on each of the charges and so working out their separate verdicts. Then the numbers of 'guilty' and 'innocent' verdicts on the charges were added up and a majority of these determined whether the final verdict would be 'guilty' or 'innocent'. Janet, then, had been found not guilty on every charge except those of having been delated of witchcraft by other witches – and the assize may have taken into account that these delations could have been motivated by malice or desperation – and of having confessed to the minister, something the assizers may have dismissed as an irrelevance or aberration in view of their decisions regarding the other charges against her.

Her proloquitor immediately asked for the documents necessary to record her innocence and have her released from prison in the tolbooth. The trial is remarkable when one takes into account its principal features. A small group of local people,

1 article Clenges

c 1 2 3 4 5 6 7 8 9 10 11 12 13 14 15
ff

2 article Clenges

c 1 2 3 4 5 6 7 8   13 15
ff   9 10 11 12   14

3 article Clenges

c   3 4   6 7   12 13 14 15
ff 1 2   5   8 9 10 11

4 article Clenges

c 1 2 3 4 5 6 7 8   11 12 13 14 15
ff   9 10

5 article Clenges

c 1 2 3 4 5 6 7 8 9 10 11 12 13 14 15
ff

6 article Clenges

c 1 2 3 4 5 6   8   14
ff   7   9 10 11 12 13   15

7 article Clenges

c 1 2 3 4 5 6 7 8 9 10 11 12 13 14 15
ff

8 article Clenges

c 1 2 3 4 5 6 7 8 9 10 11 12 13 14 15
ff

1 pairt of the 9 article
ffinds her guiltie of being delated

c 1 2 3 4 5 6 7 8 9 10 11 12 13 14 15
ff

2d pairt of the 9 article

c 1 2 3 4 5 6 7 8 9 10 11 12 13 14 15
ff

20 article
ffinds her guiltie of ane extra-judiciall confession

c
ff 1 2 3 4 5 6 7 8 9 10 11 12 13 14 15

Record of voting by the assize in the case of Janet Cock.

motivated to some extent by personal grievance, collaborated in accusing Janet of practising witchcraft. Some of the incidents in which she was involved include the death of adults and children. She had the reputation of being a witch, a reputation which went back for at last twenty-four years, and had been delated as a witch by other witches not only in the August of her arrest but eight years previously, too, in c.1653. She herself is said to have made a voluntary confession to the minister that she was a witch. The circumambient atmosphere of the period was especially hostile to witches and witchcraft. Yet she was still acquitted. It says a great deal for the integrity of the assize and its determination to administer justice in accordance with what its members viewed as the truth of the situation, revealed by the evidence they had heard. Moreover, it may be worth bearing in mind that Janet could well have been guilty of practising some form of magic, even if she had not done so in any of the instances reported to the court. The incident of William Scott and the red-hot iron indicates that one did not have to be a witch to use magic. The verdicts upon Janet, therefore, also suggest that the assize tried her according to the evidence before them and not with prejudice.

But – and it is a pity there has to be a 'but' – the order for Janet's release leaves an ominous blank relating to the day in September on which that release was to take effect. The reason becomes clear when we look at another document dated 18 September, that is, a week after Janet's trial. She is still in the tolbooth and has sent a petition to the Justices Depute both for her release and for restoration of her property which had been seized at the time of her arrest to pay for her upkeep in prison. At the same time, however, the document records a counter-petition from the minister and kirk session of Dalkeith that she should not be set at liberty because new charges of witchcraft were going to be laid against her. The decision of the Privy Council to whom the petitions eventually made their way was, apparently, that the minister's petition should be granted and Janet tried again on this second indictment. Accordingly, warrants were issued on 8 and 9 November to the members of her first assize to re-assemble and try her once again.

Now, the fact that there was scarcely a week's interval between the end of the first trial and the issuing of a warrant by the Privy Council ordering her continued detention indicates that William Calderwood, the minister, already had sufficient charges to bring against her in the event she was found innocent of the first lot. Her second trial took place only two months later, an interval which can easily be accounted for: fresh witnesses needed to be summoned, the Court of Justiciary had a full timetable and 11 November was the earliest date it could find for the new trial, and the bureaucracy of the period tended to be slow and somewhat cumbersome. A two-month delay, therefore, was actually quite short under the circumstances.

There were twelve fresh charges against Janet. They reveal extensive quarrelling with members of her community, caused at least in part, it is clear, because people kept on calling her a witch – a perfectly understandable accusation since we know, as they did, that Janet had been practising magic over a very long period and was employed on occasion to lift an illness which seemed to have been caused by enchantment. None of this is unusual. One can see the pattern in most of the other cases of witchcraft which came before the courts.

The twelve charges can be divided into two groups. Group A consists of five items and encompasses two cures from sickness, two illnesses allegedly caused by Janet, one of which ended in death, and an incident in which plough-horses were stung by a bee or a wasp and bolted, breaking the plough in pieces during their flight. The insect, it was maintained, was sent by Janet after she and the ploughman, Alexander Smaill, had quarrelled, the occasion of their outfall being that he called her a witch and threw a heavy plate in her face. Group B is more diverse. Two people, one a child, fell sick and died; a nurse's milk dried up; a cow gave blood instead of milk; horses fell sick, and a man lost money during a business venture. Tacked on to the end is a charge by William Calderwood, the minister, that Janet had been delated as a witch by another confessing witch, and had long had the reputation of being a witch herself.

I have divided the charges thus because once again we have a detailed record of the way each of the fifteen members of the assize voted on each article of the dittay. Group A consists of those items on which a majority found Janet guilty, and Group B of those items on which most assizers found her innocent.

What this means is that Janet was acquitted of two deaths – one of them a child's – but found guilty of a third. She was found guilty of curing two people by magic and of making Alexander Smaill's horses bolt and wreck his plough. But she was acquitted of making some people and some horses ill, of drying up a nurse's milk, of causing a cow to give blood, and of causing a man to lose money in a bad business deal. There is no consistent pattern here, no automatic anger at the death of a child, for example, and indeed the voting of the assize reveals a wide divergence of opinion. One man acquitted her of all charges; no one found her guilty of all of them. In fact, only six of the fifteen found her guilty of half or more of the items on her dittay. There could be no clearer indication of the level-headedness of the assize and its concern to judge Janet fairly, honestly, and with due regard for truth.

Articles

	1	2	3	4	5	6	7	8	9	10	11	12
Andrew Haliburton	ff	c	c	c	c	c	c	c	c	c	c	c
Thomas Dick	ff	ff	ff	ff	c	c	ff	c	ff	ff	ff	ff
John Boyd	ff	c	ff	ff	c	c	ff	c	ff	ff	ff	ff
Thomas Dobie	ff	c	c	ff	c	c	ff	ff	ff	ff	ff	ff
David Livingstone	ff	c	c	ff	c	c	c	c	ff	c	ff	ff
Gilbert Hood	ff	c	c	c	c	c	c	c	ff	c	c	ff
Archibald Johnstone	c	c	ff	c	c	c	c	c	ff	c	ff	ff
John Veatch	ff	c	ff	ff	c	c	ff	ff	ff	ff	ff	ff
John Handyside	c	c	c	c	c	c	c	c	c	c	ff	ff
John Forsyth	ff	c	c	ff	c	c	c	c	c	c	ff	ff
Henry Hutchison	ff	c	c	ff	c	c	c	c	ff	c	ff	ff
John Simpson	ff	c	ff	ff	c	c	ff	ff	ff	ff	ff	ff
Henry Mitchell	c	c	c	ff	c	c	c	c	c	c	ff	c
Robert Hamilton	c	c	c	c	c	c	c	c	c	c	c	c
John Didup	ff	c	c	ff	c	c	ff	ff	c	c	ff	ff
[Final total]	ff	c	c	ff	c	c	c	c	ff	c	ff	ff

Still, the sad fact of the matter is that, in spite of the heroic efforts of her proloquitor, a majority of the assize found her guilty of five of the charges, and although that number of results amounted to fewer than half the total number of items, this plurality of voices was enough to condemn her to death. Perhaps the court was swayed by the knowledge that this was her second trial and that enough had been discovered of her guilt during the first to swing the balance of opinion against her on this occasion. A decree of condemnation was issued against her on 12 November, the day after her trial, sentencing her to the usual penalty suffered by those found guilty of witchcraft in Scotland – strangulation, burning of the dead body, and confiscation of all property. We have no actual record of the execution, but it is almost certain that the sentence would have been carried out, either in Dalkeith whence she came, or on Castle Hill in Edinburgh, within a matter of two or three days after doom had been pronounced.

If one is to look for a villain in the piece, perhaps one should scrutinize William Calderwood, the minister, or William Scott, the town baillie. Janet's second trial took place at the instance of William Calderwood, supported by the elders of his kirk, and it is interesting that at this second trial he seems to have made no mention of Janet's confession to him that she was a witch. Since the assize had discounted this in September, there was no point in using it again, and one may note that the assize of November ignored his evidence that Janet had been delated by another witch and had long been considered a witch herself. Both these accusations were obviously true, but in passing over them in silence the assize gives the impression of considering that they had been made out of personal malice, and its silence therefore looks like an oblique rebuke to both the minister and the elders.

William Scott, on the other hand, may have been a weightier and more influential figure. The Scott family of Dalkeith was almost certainly related in some fashion to the earls of

Buccleuch who held castles and lands in the area, and Janet had had more than one brush with the town baillie, a substantial figure in the community. It is possible that he was annoyed by Janet's first acquittal and determined to get her convicted if he could. Certainly he was in an ideal position to do so, even without any Buccleuch connection, and if he knew (as he would have done) that William Calderwood was irritated by the long presence and activity of a practising witch within his parish, it would not have been difficult for the two of them to combine and produce both circumstance and evidence for a second trial which they could hope would go better for them than the first. Arrangements for some such eventuality had clearly been made in advance. One does not whip up twelve extra charges and their requisite witnesses in a matter of only a week.

Janet's daughters were not in any doubt that their mother had been the victim of a concerted attempt to do away with her. They blamed the baillie. In August, after their mother's arrest and imprisonment and before her first trial, they wrote a letter of petition to the justices in Edinburgh.

The humble petition of Mary and Janet Coldanes, lawful daughters to Janet Cock, prisoner, humbly sheweth that whereas our mother, being delated by a witch whose name is Janet Paiston, and by all appearance it was out of malice and wrath, for never any but she could say or lay anything to her charge but now: since they have laid hands upon her there is many enemies raised against her that was friends to her formerly, and all for their own ends because that they do see that Baillie Scott (who did profess to be her friend till he did see what money and goods she had), now hath seized upon all she hath and is become her utter enemy. And doth not only take it upon himself to take away her life, but goeth to all and sundry whom ever he did know that had any spite or envy at our mother, and persuades them to do according to his direction. And the people, being not sensible of what they do, is afraid of him because he is head in the town [and] doth what they can to speak untruth for pleasure of him against our mother. And whereas they do know that your petitioners hath not money nor nothing else to employ no advocate nor agent to speak for our mother, nor hath no friends to do anything for us, and that all our mother and we have is in Baillie Scott's hand: it doth make both him and those who were your honours' petitioners' friends turn aways to your honours' petitioners.

It is informed by your honours' petitioners that Baillie Scott is to lay the death of a child to our mother's charge. But will it please your honours to know he had five other children dead? Your honours may ask who was the death of them. There is one Elizabeth Pringle that had her [Janet Cock] at envy. She would have had her house over her head, and my mother not willing to remove out of the house at that time, she sayeth she did her harm now. But before it was never mentioned. And there was a drunken woman that was drunk one night, that did scold with our mother, and our mother did warn her before the church, and the minister and own session did make that woman ask our mother forgiveness: and they were ever friends till this time. And now Baillie Scott hath put all these people against her. And moreover will it please your honours, this day he hath said that he shall not have a groat in the world but he shall have her burned, and only because we have taken upon us to petition to your honours that justice may be done to her, and not to let her lie in pain.

It is a touching document which has the ring of truth about it. So were Mary and Janet correct in their assertions? A look at the decisions reached by the two assizes at their mother's trials suggests that there is at least a possibility they were, and that Janet Cock was unlucky not to have achieved a second as well as a first 'not guilty' verdict.

—❦ CHAPTER FIVE ❧—

Neither Gone Nor Forgotten

Janet Cock's trials happened towards the end of what one might call the period of intensive bursts of prosecution for witchcraft in Western Europe, and it is timely to ask why this persecutory period should have happened at all. The simple answer is, we do not know. Several different explanations are attractive and each has a degree of validity up to a point, but none is sufficient in itself.

Certain Catholic territories – Trier, Mainz, Bamberg, Württemberg, for example – saw powerful individuals turning their personal preoccupations with sin and Satan's power upon earth into a drive to eliminate the Devil's human helpers, and these have been blamed for initiating and pursuing hunts to what was sometimes an alarming degree of ferocity. But it is equally important in dealing with these same areas to investigate their attendant socio-economic circumstances, such as epidemics, rises in the price of grain, unusually high mortality among children, crop failures, and similar misfortunes or catastrophes which seemed to inflict themselves on the population with unexpected frequency or unusual severity. What is more, for every Johann Christoph whose zeal set off the panics which disfigured Ellwangen at the beginning of the seventeenth century, one can summon evidence for the calming influence of a central government, as in the case of the intervention by Innsbruck in the prosecutions of 1595-1602 in the Habsburg County of Hohenberg.

It has also been suggested that small cities with weak governments tended to produce high numbers of prosecutions. Yet exceptions may be found, such as Mainz which had a strong centralized authority but continued to prosecute witches heavily until the arrival of Swedish armies in 1631 put an end to the self-perpetuating cycle; and an examination of Reutlingen has indicated that with each generational change in the city's governing élites – roughly a thirty-year period – witch-prosecution broke out with renewed violence as younger men sought to dislodge their elders from office and used pursuit of witches as a means of ingratiating themselves with the public. A third explanation says that conflict with one's neighbours provided a constant spur to alleviate one's troubles and solve apparently intractable problems (whether material or psychological) by accusing them of bewitching oneself, one's family and animals, or one's goods. Research from the Netherlands, however, has shown that, in the province of Drenthe, accusations of witchcraft were not preceded by any such strife with neighbours. A fourth suggestion, which blames a misogynistic patriarchal society for widescale murderous attacks upon women, tends to depend upon a careful selection of the available evidence, and makes the fundamental mistake of presuming that witches were prosecuted because they were women rather than because they were witches and therefore breakers of a law. This suggestion also more or less ignores the role of male and infant witches, whose numbers are by no means negligible, and offers little or no explanation of their presence as victims in the supposed patriarchal conspiracy against wives, daughters, and sisters.

Quot homines, tot sententiae says the Latin tag: 'There are as many opinions as there are people', and this certainly has a ring of truth when applied to explanations for the onset of intensive witchcraft prosecution. Certain factors, however, need to be taken into consideration, regardless of which explanation one tends to favour. I have already mentioned socio-economic conditions. Neighbourly conflict was certainly widespread, but work still needs to be done to investigate the nature of these disagreements in any given place and time – it is remarkable, for example, how little Satan has to do with any of them and how infrequently he figures in the evidence brought before the courts – and religious partisanship or animus is also a major factor. Both the Catholic and the various Protestant Churches wanted to eradicate those remnants of pagan (or, in the case of Protestants, Catholic) belief and practice which they considered to be harmful to spiritual progress or reformation, and which they both increasingly called 'superstition', but neither side was averse from using aspects of magic (such as demonic possession), as propaganda against its religious opponents. Did the very attention paid by churchmen to magic of any kind actually help to prolong a belief among the populace that the subject must still be important in spite of the Church's fulminations against it, because her priests and ministers quite clearly treated it with immense seriousness?

When it came to the business of ceasing to prosecute witches, there were equally wide variations in practice and explanation. Zeeland, for example, does not seem to have prosecuted witches (as opposed to other types of magical practitioner), let alone executed them, after about 1565, whereas Switzerland executed its last witch in 1782. But the worst of the outbreaks can be seen within the period c.1580–c.1665, with individual or small groups of cases ranging before and after it. These outbreaks had never taken place over a whole country, of course. It is an error to suppose that any particular country saw its government consciously or deliberately conducting mass efforts to eradicate magical operators, including witches, the length and breadth of its jurisdiction, even if Voltaire, in a dramatic generalization, did describe France in relation to trials for witchcraft as 'one vast theatre of judicial carnage'.[1] Trials and executions were principally of one or two individuals, accused by other individuals from their own communities and brought to their local administrative or legal centre to underlie the law for their alleged crime. It is only when large numbers of these trials occur within a relatively short space of time, or when trials initially involving single numbers see a rapid multiplication of secondary, third, and fourth ripples of accusation stemming from one another that we can justifiably say that something like a 'panic' has taken place.

Moreover, when we read of the last reported execution of a witch – 1643 in Malines, Belgium; 1699 in Estonia; 1711 in Ireland; 1722 in Denmark; 1727 in Scotland; 1756 in Austria – we are not necessarily reading about the last deaths for witchcraft, only about the last cases in which these occurred legally. Lynchings might as well have continued, as in the Landes de Gascogne, until the early decades of the nineteenth century, or suspected witches might have died during attempts to destroy their powers by water or by fire, as in the case of the Irish woman, Bridget Cleary, who was killed in 1895, perhaps inadvertently, by her husband and a number of female and male relatives during repeated efforts to drive out a demonic or fairy personality which had replaced the genuine Bridget.

A common approach to the subject-matter, therefore, has been to assume that during the second half of the seventeenth century, and certainly during the eighteenth, 'rationality' broke into the dark chambers of Europe's collective 'superstition' and let in the light of scientific explanation for everything. The age of Locke, Hobbes, and Voltaire (it is assumed) put paid to belief in the validity of witchcraft which then retreated into the depths of the countryside where it stagnated and became one of the peculiar characteristics of ignorant peasants, or dwindled into a harmless remnant of rustic folklore. In fact, this assumption does not even begin to be true. But it has led to a general neglect of the later period among historians of witchcraft and the occult sciences, and thus badly distorted their overall view of the subject by encouraging them to concentrate on the period of the witch-trials. So an unacknowledged assumption that the end of the trials and executions for witchcraft coincided with the end of a belief, if only among the educated, in witchcraft itself has tended to lead people to take at face value the exclamatory and often condescending claims of the scribbling classes to represent the ethos and *mores* of their time. In fact (as is quite commonly the case), they represented no one except them-selves, and tracing and accounting for the actual beliefs of the general populace is a more interesting and rewarding task than listening to the self-congratulatory scepticism of a few.

Still, it was the educated who formed the legislatures which repealed existing statutes forbidding the practice of magic and witchcraft, or forbade prosecution of such practitioners in future. Nevertheless, the motives of these legislators were not entirely stimulated by scepticism. In July 1682, France, for example, saw the promulgation of a royal edict by Louis XIV, which reclassi-fied divination, magic, and enchantment as forms of superstition, and sought to punish their practitioners as frauds, a turnabout which may suggest that it was scepticism which lay behind the King's decision. Exception, however, was made in the decree for any who practised such 'superstitions' in tandem with impiety, sacrilege, or poisoning, and it is this exception which provides us with a clue to the real stimulus for the decree. For between 1676 and 1681 the Court and the upper reaches of Parisian society had been both shocked and entertained by *l'affaire des poisons*, a series of magical activities involving poison, infanticide, blasphemy, sacrilege, and love-magic, all perpetrated at the instance of the King's current mistress, Madame de Montespan, with the assistance of a dubious 'witch' known as La Voisin.

La Voisin was no ordinary magician. Claiming that 'only another God can understand my powers', she presided with a carefully calculated theatricality over séances and magical ceremonies held in her apartments in the rue Beauregard to which *tout Paris* flocked in ever-increasing numbers. Indeed, so famous did she become that Thomas Corneille and Donneau de Visé wrote a spoof inspired by her career, *La Devineresse*, which had a four-month run at the Théâtre de Guénégaud between November 1679 and February 1680. The affair which put paid to her career involved the very highest in France. La Montespan, fearful that she might be losing the King's favour, turned to La Voisin for help which was provided, in part, by sacrilegious Masses celebrated by a renegade priest upon La Montespan's naked body (forerunners of the so-called 'Black Masses' of popular imagination). During one of these, according to the later testimony of Voisin's step-daughter, an infant, clearly premature, was brought in and had its throat cut over the chalice. The body was taken away and incinerated, while the entrails were preserved, distilled, and combined with other ingredients to form a magic potion which La Montespan picked up the following day and took away with her.

These Masses, however, were only the most histrionic of La Voisin's methods. During her subsequent interrogations by Nicolas Gabriel de la Reynie, newly appointed Procurateur Général of Police, she admitted to carrying out abortions (many of which will have taken place according to the exigencies of her magical practice), and said that the ashes of as many as 25,000 infants had been scattered over the garden of her villa not far from the Saint-Denis gate of Paris. When her house in rue Beauregard was searched, a large selection of items, mainly poisonous, was discovered in a locked cabinet. Upstairs in cupboards the searchers found grimoires (books of magical instruction), priestly vestments, black candles, and incense: and in a stove in the garden, fragments of children's bones among the ashes. Assistants to La Voisin specialized in poisons and aphrodisiacs based upon such ingredients as frogs' tongues, cocks' testicles, and Spanish fly. Powders concocted from these and similar items made their way into La Montespan's household, clearly intended for ingestion by the King himself.

When these and all the other horrific details of the case came to light under La Reynie's diligent scrutiny, that same tout Paris which had beaten a track to La Voisin's door now took delight in savouring the story and attending her execution. In all, nearly 400 people were arrested, and when the courts had finished hearing the evidence, thirty-six people were executed, five sent to the galleys, and twenty-three banished. Madame de Sévigné, as it happened, was among the crowd which witnessed La Voisin's death, and wrote a brief account of it to her daughter and son-in-law the following day, 21 February 1680:

On Thursday, which was yesterday...she was brought in a carriage from Vincennes to Paris. She had a slight choking fit and was embarrassed by it. They wanted her to confess, but I cannot tell you anything further about that. At five o'clock, they bound her and she appeared in the tumbril, carrying a torch in her hand. She was dressed in white, the traditional mode of attire in which one is burned. She was very flushed, and it was noticed she violently pushed away the confessor and the crucifix... At Notre Dame she absolutely refused to apologise for what she had done, and at the Place de Grève struggled as much as she could to prevent herself from being removed from the tumbril. They dragged her out of it by force, put her on the pyre, sat her down, bound her to the stake with irons, and covered her with straw. She swore a great deal and pushed aside the straw five or six times. At last, however, the fire spread and she was lost to sight. Her ashes are still hanging in the air.

The affair of the poisons, then, involved precisely those activities condemned by Louis XIV's decree of 1682. Like James VI of Scotland who had been the focal point of magical conspiracies nearly a hundred years before, Louis was badly frightened and this fear reveals itself not so much in the penalties levied against anyone who might combine magic with poison and blasphemy – what else, it is reasonable to ask, might one expect? – as in the reclassification of divination, magic, and enchantment as superstitious nonsense. Far from being an example of the advance of rationalism, Louis's edict seems to have been an emotional attempt to draw the sting of the King's fear by claiming that there was no reality, no validity behind what La Voisin and her accomplices had been doing and what Madame de Montespan and a great number of educated, sophisticated aristocrats and bourgeois had been asking them to do. Let us make no mistake, these people were not playing at magic. When they asked La Voisin for help, they expected realities, not play-acting. Rationality, then, it seems to me, does not enter the picture.

Contrast this with Britain where repeal of the Scottish Witchcraft Act of 1563 and the English Act of 1604 was passed simultaneously by the Westminster Parliament of 1736. The stimuli for this have been traced to a number of different, though interlocking causes. First may be mentioned marked changes in the religious sensibilities of the seventeenth century, which saw a developing rationalist theology combine with Cartesian philosophy to push God to a remote eminence beyond the workings of nature in which it was proposed he played little active part. The civil wars in Scotland and England, it has been suggested, produced a reaction against religious enthusiasm – hence the growing interest in rationalist theology – and a new view of society, which saw it less as an ordered unity of which the world of witchcraft was a frightening inversion, and more as a loose coalition of different groups and factions. The Puritan language of providentialism, which had helped to sustain the intellectual and theological discourse of a negative society such as witchcraft provided, faded before the increasing desire for 'reasonableness', and 'reasonable' men found themselves uneasy in the face of witchcraft theory which posited a view of the workings of God and nature they no longer found comfortable or convincing.

Yet there was also deep concern expressed by others over an apparent growth in scepticism, and its attendant social secularization, among those whom Joseph Glanvill characterized in 1681 as 'the looser Gentry, and the small pretenders to Philosophy and wit', which the more orthodox interpreted as an inclination to atheism. As John Wesley wrote in 1768, 'the giving up of witchcraft is in effect giving up the Bible', and he went on to record his feelings at greater length in his journal:

> The infidels have hooted witchcraft out of the world; and the complaisant Christians, in large numbers, have joined with them in the cry. I do not so much wonder at this, that many of these should herein talk like infidels; but I have sometimes been inclined to wonder at the pert, saucy, indecent manner wherein some of those trample upon men far wiser than themselves; at their speaking so dogmatically against what not only the world, Heathen and Christian, believed in all past ages, but thousands, learned as well as unlearned, firmly believe at this day.
>
> *Journal*, 1 July 1770

Evidently public and even learned opinion was divided into factions whose beliefs we must not try to pin down with too nice a precision. Rather we should place them upon a continuum ranging from continuing belief in the earlier world-view which accommodated, and indeed presupposed the validity of magic, to the rejection of such a view in favour of those explanations of unexpected occurrences, disease, and personal misfortune provided by natural science and the psycho-physiological theories of eighteenth-century medicine. But if the latter represents the prevailing climate in certain circles, especially in Edinburgh and London, the former also exercised an important sway in Scotland where a still dominant Presbyterian establishment fought fiercely against any suggestion that witches were not capable of real preternatural malevolence, and that the penalties prescribed by law to counter their dangerous activity should in any way be curtailed.

1 Above left: *Bound female figure representing an evil spirit, from Mesopotamia.*

2 Above right: *A doll prepared for erotic magic.*

3 Above: *A defixio.*

4 *A white and grey hunting owl. The term 'strix', meaning screech-owl, was also used to denote a witch who changed her shape into that of a bird.*

5 *The archangel Gabriel spearing the evil eye.*

6 *The magical cosmos.*

7 Top and middle: *Two engravings showing the Devil carrying off a damned woman.*

8 Below left: *Magical archery, from Molitor's* De lamiis at phitonicis mulieribus.

9 Below right: *Père Lafitau's drawings of Amerindian musical instruments.*

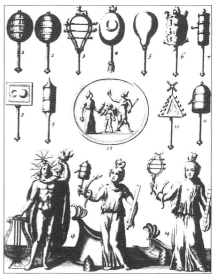

10 *Botticelli's* Mystical Nativity.

11 *The 'demon' Pachacamac talking to Indians in Peru.*

12 *The different stages of a witch's flight to the Sabbat.*

13 Left and opposite: *Two depictions of witches as ugly old crones: (a) A witch and her demon attendant; (b) Woodcut of the Witch of Newbury, 1643.*

A MOST
Certain, Strange, and true Discovery of a
VVITCH.

Being taken by some of the Parliament Forces, as she was
standing on a small planck board and sayling on
it over the River of *Newbury*:

Together with the strange and true manner of her death, with
the propheticall words and speeches she vsed at the same time.

Printed by John Hammond, 1643.

14 Clockwise from top left: *Less stereotyped views of witches:*
(a) A witch and a winged devil;
(b) Fashionably dressed witches at a Sabbat;
(c) Anne Bodenham working magic, 1688.

15 Above: Circe, *Dosso Dossi*.

16 From top: *(a) Satan's baptism; (b) A male witch receiving the Devil's mark; (c) Witches rifling graves.*

17 From top: *(a) Witches offering a child to Satan; (b) Witches dancing with demons; (c) Witches roasting a child.*

18 Above left: Che Vuoi?

19 Above right: Allá va eso, *Goya.*

20 Opposite: The Witches' Sabbat, *Goya.*

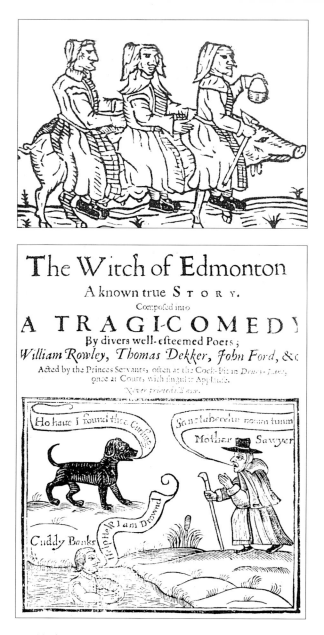

21 (a) Three witches travelling on a pig, 1612; (b) Mother Sawyer, 1658.

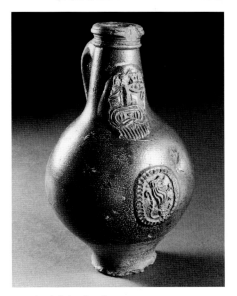

22 *A witch-bottle, 1650-1700.*

23 *A curse-doll, probably early nineteenth-century.*

24 *Tam o' Shanter pursued by a witch.*

So late as the year 1785 [wrote Hugo Arnot] it was the custom among the sect of Seceders to read from the pulpit an annual confession of sins, national and personal; amongst the former of which was particularly mentioned the Repeal by parliament of the penal statute against witches, contrary to the express laws of God.

A Collection and Abridgement of Celebrated
Criminal Trials in Scotland, 1785

Repeal of the two British Witchcraft Acts was therefore more or less a unilateral decision by Westminster. Evidence for the emergence of the legislation is, unfortunately, sparse, but we know that the 1735-6 Parliament devoted itself largely to Church matters and that anticlericalism was rife as a result of factionalism within the establishment élite. Witchcraft theory had been adopted as a propaganda tool by the Tories, the political grouping (perhaps one should not say 'party' at this stage) which had been in the ascendant under Queen Anne and had now lost its place to the Whigs under the new Hanoverian dispensation. The Repeal Bill itself was thus sponsored by Whigs, one of whom, George Heathcote, was anticlerical to a degree and notable for the violence of his oratory and sympathy to republicanism – a man almost bound to attract opposition in equal measure.

This came from a Scotsman, George Erskine, younger brother of the earl of Mar. Erskine was a fervent Presbyterian, unambiguous in his belief in the operation of divine grace in the world, and the reality of the Devil and his use of human agents to further his wicked purposes. During the 1730s there had been political abrasiveness between the Scots and the English in Westminster, and Erskine had been vocal in his insistence upon preservation of Scottish rights and Scottish distinctiveness in the face of what he perceived as attacks upon them. If we are to believe the tendentious account of a liberal cleric, Alexander Carlyle, who was an avid hater of Erskine and all he stood for, when Erskine stood up in the Commons to speak against the Bill, his speech (and it was his maiden speech, too) was not received seriously but with 'a Titter of laughter'.

It is important, too, that we bear in mind the symbolic use to which witchcraft could be put. For the French in particular – headed by Voltaire and the *philosophes* – attacks on 'superstition' of all kinds were to a large degree cloaks for assaults upon Catholicism and the Catholic Church. The executions of a number of Huguenots in 1762 and 1764, for example, caused Voltaire to write a pamphlet, ostensibly directed towards rehabilitating these unfortunates, but also aimed more broadly at the evils stemming from what he perceived as fanaticism. As parallel examples, Voltaire adduced the past history of the European witchcraft trials, which he attributed to ignorance and the fanaticism of Catholic clerics. 'The more a province was ignorant and uncouth, the more it acknowledged the dominion of the Devil', he said, and meanwhile the Church imagined she could force people to accept her orthodoxy 'by never ceasing to stir them up by means of the most appalling slanders, by persecuting them, and by dragging them to the galleys, to the gallows, on to the wheel, and into the flames'.[2]

In England, the same spirit of anti-Catholicism was often reproduced. Stories about ghosts and witches, observed the author of *Cato's Letters* in 1722,

> are believed through the world, in exact proportion to the ignorance of the people, and the integrity of their clergy, and the influence they have over their flocks. In Popish countries there is a spirit or witch

in every parish, in defiance of holy water, and of constant *pater nosters*; and there are more of them in ignorant Popish countries than in knowing ones.

No. 79, 2 June

These sentiments were nothing new. They were part of a long polemic tradition (not peculiar to England, for the same kind of thing can be seen and read in German literature of this and an earlier period) in which Protestant writers on the one hand emphasized the role of the Devil as a spiritual entity aiming its force against the individual soul and conscience, while on the other presenting older conceptions of him as a physical, often frightening or lurid creature, in literature intended to make Protestant propaganda or score confessional points.

So we can suggest that repeal of the Witchcraft Acts was carried for a variety of reasons. One is faction: if the Tories were against repeal, the Whigs would be for it; if clerical supporters were for it, anticlerical opinion would be against it. Another is confessional bias: magic and witchcraft were regularly associated with an historical period of Catholic domination on the continent of Europe, and a myth was being created and fostered that Catholic countries were backward-looking as opposed to Protestant countries which looked to the future – some perhaps more than others, for, as the *Cato Letter* I quoted earlier observed with smug (and entirely inaccurate) satisfaction, '[in] England...no clergymen of any credit abet these frauds; and consequently the Devil's empire here is almost at an end'. Another reason may be personal antipathy (and one should never ignore or underestimate emotion in historical actions which depend upon snap decisions reached in a heady atmosphere): a reaction against a supporter of the Acts who was not well liked; who had embarrassed or irritated the House with the vehemence of his pleading for a world-view, which many MPs – subscribing to the new forms of scepticism prevalent in certain quarters at the time – would have found superstitious and old-fashioned; and who was a Scot in a Parliament dominated by English who had memories of his own and his brother's part in the rebellion of 1715, and even more recent memories of Erskine's stout defence of Scottish rights against creeping English assaults upon them.

The notion of scepticism in relation to magic and witchcraft during this period should also be treated with caution, if only because one needs to define the term before embarking on a discussion of it. 'Scepticism' may refer, for example, not to the validity of the magical world-view as a whole, but to doubts concerning the reality or possibility of certain magical operations. From medieval times there was a running debate over whether witches could and did really fly to the Sabbat or whether their reports of such flights stemmed from diabolical illusion or an imbalance of the humours resulting in what we should now call temporary psychological disturbance. Thus, John Webster wrote in 1677,

And as there are a numerous crew of active witches, whose existence we freely acknowledge; so there are another sort, that are under a passive delusion, and know not, or at least do not observe or understand, that they are deluded or imposed upon. These are those that confidently believe that they see, do, and suffer many strange, odd, and wonderful things, which have indeed no existence at all in them, but only in their depraved fancies, and are merely *melancholiae figmenta*. And yet the confessions of these, though absurd, idle, foolish, false, and impossible, are without all ground and reason by the common Witchmongers taken to be truths, and falsely ascribed unto Demons, and that they are sufficient grounds to proceed upon to condemn the Confessors to death, when all is but passive delusion, intrinsically wrought in the deprived imaginative faculty.

The Displaying of Suppos'd Witchcraft

'Scepticism' may also encompass people's realization that trickery could be involved in what they saw, as in the case of Anne Gunter who, in 1604, claimed she had been bewitched by other women (whom she named) from her community. Close investigation of her allegations at the time, however, revealed that she had been put up to it by her father who bore a grudge against relatives of one of the women Anne was accusing, and that her vomitings of strange objects such as pins, her convulsions, her manic rages, and the other symptoms of demonic possession which she displayed were, in fact, either pieces of deliberate theatre or physical reactions to drugged drinks her father was forcing her to take.

Thirdly, 'scepticism' may involve doubts about the magical world-view itself. One of its most thorough dismissals was penned by an English country gentleman, Reginald Scot, in 1584, but his *Discoverie of Witchcraft* is not as straightforward a work of modernizing doubt as it may appear at a first or rapid reading. For the principal thrust of his book, supported by a remarkable knowledge of the Bible and the Church Fathers, is anti-Catholicism in particular and anti-clericalism in general. Scot (like a good Protestant, but not necessarily the Puritan he is often made out to be) is eager to ensure that nothing stand in the way of a direct relationship between human beings and God, and because the teeming spirit-world can be interpreted as just such an obstacle, he condemns and dismisses it. Satan he does not dismiss, and he acknowledges that the Devil can exercise great power in the world, but, he insists, 'the assaults of Satan are spiritual and not temporal', and therefore he cannot affect people's bodies nor enter into the kind of covenant with a human as is suggested by the theory of the witch's pact. Thus the *Discoverie* is a Protestant work of controversy intended partly to alert its readers to what Scot sees as the cozening danger and false religion embodied in the Catholic faith, and partly to plead for an end to what he regards as the mistaken, distracting view of creation as a world peopled with malevolent spirits whose human agents must be identified and eradicated. His condemnation of the prosecution and punishment of witches is therefore rooted in contemporary religious argument and not 'scientific' or proto-Enlightenment scepticism.

The scepticism of those who expressed a view on magic and witchcraft, then, needs to be examined carefully and related to its context. Nor should it be supposed that magic and witchcraft were subjects solely for religious debate. One of the most important uses to which both were put was in the curing of illnesses, and so we must expect physicians to have had opinions about their role in the healing process. As with theologians, doctors differed in their attitudes to the extent of diabolical power over physical or mental disability. Thomas Willis, for example, accepted that certain illnesses could be ascribed to magical or demonic causation, but drew the line at others:

> That convulsive distempers are sometimes excited by witchcraft, is both commonly believed and usually affirmed by many Authors worthy of Credit: and indeed, as we do grant that very often-times most admirable passions are produced in the humane body by the delusions of the Devil ... yet all kinds of convulsions, which besides

the common manner of this disease [epilepsy] appear prodigious, ought not presently to be attributed to the enchantments of Witches, nor is the Devil presently or always to be brought upon the stage.

A Medical Philosophical Discourse on Fermentation

The German doctor, Daniel Sennert, however, denied preternatural intervention altogether, and appealed to the powers of the imagination as the source of certain physical difficulties.

Nothing acts beyond the abilities inherent in its own species. Similarly, it is a mistake to claim that witches can induce impotence by tying things together, locking doors, and so forth, or by mumbling some words. One may make an exception in the case of a man who is inclined to superstition and who, through the workings of his own imagination, may easily impede or encourage the flow of those spirits which are needed to enlarge the penis. As for those who have just been married, these people are often bound and restrained from performing the marital act by a sense of embarrassment. But experience and familiarity will loosen and restore their sexual potency.

Physica Hypomnemata, 1637

Whether the physician was prepared to concede a degree of diabolical interference or not, however, his caution was usually heeded only by members of his own profession or others similarly educated. When it came to his patients, magic still held its old tenacious sway. 'Say what you can,' complained John Webster,

they shall not believe you, but account you a physician of small or no value, and whatsoever you do to them, it shall hardly do them any

good at all, because of the fixedness of their depraved and prepos-
sessed imagination. But if you indulge their fancy, and hang any
insignificant thing about their necks, assuring them that it is a most
efficacious and powerful charm, you may settle their imaginations,
and then give them that which is proper to eradicate the cause of
their disease, and so you may cure them, as we have done in great
numbers.

The Displaying of Suppos'd Witchcraft

This lack of comprehension across the educational and class
divide continued at least to the margins of the twentieth
century, but as magic and witchcraft in the post-prosecution
centuries have only just begun to receive scholarly attention, our
ability to synthesize information and to draw comparisons
between one country, or even region, and another is somewhat
limited.

Thanks to the pioneering work of Owen Davies, however,
England is one of the best-studied countries for the later period.
In *Witchcraft, Magic and Culture, 1736-1951*, Davies not only
presents a wealth of evidence to show that magic in all its forms
was being practised there well into the twentieth century, but
also makes a number of general points which, *mutatis mutandis*,
have a direct bearing on the study of other places and are
therefore well worth repeating here:

(i) During the sixteenth and seventeenth centuries, those in
authority actively sought to change popular beliefs and eradicate
practices they deemed superstitious or otherwise undesirable.
During the eighteenth and nineteenth centuries, however, this
zeal for reform changed to disdain, and the educated now
withdrew the hems of their skirts from attitudes and operations
they claimed to find ridiculous and irritating. [It is a change

which represents an interesting psychological split in society, and I am reminded of changes in the living-arrangements of the citizens of Edinburgh symbolized, perhaps, by the building of the New Town there from 1767 onwards. Until then, the classes had lived more or less cheek by jowl in the tall apartment blocks of the Old Town enduring, as best they might, each other's foibles and vices. But once the New Town started to appear, this proximity evaporated and with it the subliminal sympathy and traditional bonds which had existed, however imperfectly, hitherto.]

(ii) Rural communities lost their stability as first agricultural, then industrial change affected them. Witchcraft had been directed largely against domestic targets – the various aspects of the home economy such as butter or cheese making, the health of humans and animals – but now butter and cheese were often taken out of the hands of individuals and turned over to factory production. Insurance meant that the loss, say, of a cow or a horse, or a sudden protracted illness in the family, was not necessarily quite the financial disaster it had been in previous centuries, and hence the targets of potential witchcraft appeared to be less at risk.

(iii) Local communities also started to lose their traditional forms of self-government. Thus, the minister and village elders played less and less of a policing role as a new, professional police force established itself, bringing national government into small communities in a way they had not seen or experienced before. What is more, these new figures of authority were not subject, as their predecessors had been, to local ties of obligation or kinship, and were therefore less likely to turn a blind eye to breaches of the law, such as ducking or swimming a person suspected or openly accused of being a witch.

(iv) In spite of what nineteenth-century clergymen and folk-lorists claimed, magic and witchcraft had not disappeared from towns and cities to become a quaint remnant in the more primitive reaches of village and countryside. Cities themselves, despite their rapid growth under frequent waves of immigration, settled their populations not into one amorphous mass but into small communities forming an interlocked network of urban villages. Where that analogy breaks down, of course, is in the nature of the networking both within and between those urban communities. Because of the ebb and flow of individuals into and out of the neighbourhood, people had no real chance to build up a long, intimate knowledge of their neighbours and in consequence even if they suspected that one of them was prac-tising witchcraft to their personal detriment, they might well hesitate to initiate a prosecution because they could not be certain how everyone else would react. When prosecutions did occur, therefore, they tended to be directed less against neigh-bours and more against members of the prosecutor's own family. So it is not that magic and witchcraft disappeared from cities, but that they operated in ways different from those employed in the countryside.

(v) Davies's most important observation concerns the decrease in witchcraft prosecutions during this later period. It has become the habit to maintain that this happened as a result of a decline in belief in witchcraft. Davies, however, offers substantial evidence to suggest that in England at any rate it was actually the other way round. The fewer witchcraft prosecutions there were, the more belief in witchcraft tended to decline since, as he says, 'once out of sight, the witch was very much out of mind'. Education, however, in which both eighteenth- and nineteenth-century authorities placed much faith as the principal tool whereby new men and women would be honed into modern products, freed from the spiritual excrescences of ignorance and superstition which had disfigured their lives in the past, did not work as it was intended. Increased literacy, indeed, often meant that people now had access to works of magic they were unable to use before.

These points are all important, but one should not omit to mention changes in legal procedure and expectation which had been occurring in some jurisdictions as long ago as the seventeenth century. Basically, the judicial system was made more efficient. The use of torture was first restricted and then prohibited, partly as the result of a flow of influential legal treatises on the subject published in the last years of the seventeenth and the early years of the eighteenth century. But it is worth noting that in most countries torture continued to be used long after their last trial for witchcraft. The last legal execution of a witch in Europe, for example, took place in Switzerland in 1782, and yet torture continued in legal use in the Swiss canton of Glarus until 1851. So in effect what happened was that the kind of restrictions the Inquisition was accustomed (if only officially) to place on the use of torture were gradually observed by non-Catholic jurisdictions. Again, legal treatises and practising judges became less and less inclined to accept the wilder forms of testimony against accused witches, and demanded much more rigorous proof of witnesses' statements. They were also increasingly reluctant to accept confessions without firm corroborative evidence from other quarters; and the tendency for doctors to psychologize certain forms of bewitchment, such as demonic possession or the effects of the evil eye, also persuaded the courts to look for explanations other than preternatural for incidents attributed to the person underlying the law. It was therefore more and more difficult, in certain places, for witchcraft prose-cutions to succeed. Failure then began to induce reluctance to prosecute, and reluctance led to indifference or resignation.

Let us be clear, therefore, that there is no simple answer to the question, why did prosecution of witches begin to cease in Western Europe during the eighteenth and nineteenth centuries? Changes in legal procedure and a growing expecta-tion that courts would be presented with more exacting standards of proof meant that frivolous or malicious accusations of witchcraft stood less chance of being heard, and even serious charges had greater difficulty in being brought to a satisfactory judicial conclusion. Legislation abolishing or curtailing prosecu-tion was passed for a variety of reasons, not many of which were directly linked to scepticism. Learned scepticism itself was often caught up in the toils of confessional animus, while priests and monks were often approached to act as unwitchers, a function they carried out unwillingly – and sometimes unknowingly, as when they gave a blessing or performed an exorcism, both of which might be perceived by the recipient as a form of unwitching.

The later period also saw many clergy begin to rely on medical rather than spiritual explanations for cases of demonic possession, and some doctors waged positive war on magical healers, dubbing their methods quackery and their motives fraudulence. Indeed, the nineteenth century in France witnessed almost frantic bellicosity between anti-clerical opponents, among whom a good many doctors numbered themselves, and religious advocates who, in the case of Lourdes, for example, found themselves divided between a defence of the heavenly visitation of Mary and the subsequent miracles at her shrine on the one hand, and on the other strong reservation and deprecation in the face of a rash of apparent visionaries and the continuation and aggrandisement of 'superstitious' beliefs and practices so much in local evidence. One can appreciate their dilemma, for in this connection it is interesting to note that Saint Bernadette chose to refer to the Virgin as 'uo pétito damizéla', the common local term for a fairy; that the religious authorities were much exercised at first in case the visions were not heavenly but diabolical in origin; and that the spring which burst forth was treated by people who visited the spot in much the same way as other magical fountains whose waters possessed curative powers. Lourdes, in fact, presented both ecclesiastical and secular authorities with a variety of problems not, to be sure, peculiar to the nineteenth century, but which the nineteenth century set out to resolve in its own particular way; and where earlier centuries would have seen the religious explanation confident in itself, the 1800s turned to 'science' for the answer to its questions.

Scepticism − whether anent the magical world-view as a whole or simply the effectiveness of some magical operations − certainly grew in educated circles, although one must not make the mistake of imagining that the educated élite ascribed to any coherent body of opinion. Attitudes towards magic were as varied among its members as they had ever been. What made scepticism more acceptable in these circles was the increasingly rapid volume of information pouring in from inventors, explorers, travellers, experimenters, astronomers and so on to which the educated had immediate access, should they want it; changes in the way society arranged itself, which made the educated self-consciously regard themselves as almost different in kind from the lower, and particularly the rural classes, so that whatever the latter believed, the former were likely to reject as both ridiculous and passé; and rationalism was replacing theology as a means of explaining the workings of creation. Not for nothing was the Goddess Reason enthroned in Paris during the French revolution as an expression both of anti-clericalism and of what revolutionary intellectuals hoped might become the new *Zeitgeist*.

'The perfectibility of society' thus threatened to take the place of God, but when the revolution turned sour and it became clear that perfectibility was not going to happen, at least in the immediate future, new avenues were explored and fresh sciences called upon to furnish their own forms of comfort. Psychiatry turned out to be one which seemed to provide satisfactory explanations for the degeneration and recidivism people thought they saw around them, and hysteria became a catch-all answer to questions of deviant or even religious behaviour. It appeared to explain not only belief in magic and witchcraft and the excesses of those demonically possessed, but also the trances and fervour of Christian saints and mystics, and the sixteenth-century German physician Johann Wier (1515-1588) was turned into a kind of godfather of psychiatry on the strength of his having taken the view that witches were people suffering from mental illness, who needed treatment rather than criminal prosecution. The newly secular or disenchanted age thus busied itself formulating myths to suit its view that the world was emerging from darkness into light, and that the future could hold only progress and improvement.

Magic and witchcraft, however, not to mention Satan and his evil spirits, did not disappear in the new light of science. But it is true that Protestant countries especially had seen a loss of the sense of the Devil as a personal – and, so to speak, physical – expression of evil. Indeed, the older notion of the witch flying to a Sabbat and there meeting and having sexual intercourse with a creature of flesh and blood, however unlike a human being he might choose to present himself, had started to disappear from witchcraft accusations during the seventeenth century. But expel Satan by the front door and he will re-enter the house through the back. Limitation of space forbids me to do more than offer a very limited sketch to illustrate this point, but it is well known that the eighteenth century saw the preter-natural flourish in both its theatre and its fiction as the very social class which prided itself on its scepticism and rationality flocked to see performances whose power was derived from a rhetoric of fear and who, in the second half of the century, read Gothic novels whose aim was to inspire a similar delighted *frisson* in the quietness of the study or drawing-room.

An impression of the period's high acting style may be gleaned from descriptions of two actresses, one French, the other English. The first comes in the form of a tribute by the great French tragedienne, La Clairon, to a fellow performer:

I remember being exceedingly unwell at a time when I had to act Ariane; and fearing that I should not be able to go through the fatigue of the character, I had caused an easy chair to be placed upon the stage, to sustain me in case I should require it. In fact, during the fifth act, while expressing my despair at the flight of Phaedra and Theseus, my strength did fail me, and I sunk almost senseless into the chair. The *intelligence* of Mademoiselle Brilland, who played my confidante, suggested to her the occupation of the scene at this moment by the most interesting attentions about me. She threw herself at my feet, took one of my hands, and bathed it with her

tears. In the speech she had to deliver, her words were slowly artic-
ulated, and interrupted by her sobs. She thus gave me time to recover
myself. Her look, her action affected me deeply; I threw myself into
her arms, and the public, in tears, acknowledged this intelligence by
the loudest applause.

J. Boaden: Memoirs of Mrs. Siddons, 2.66–7

Realism, as we understand it, was not required, and the
audience fully participated, not so much in a willing suspension
of disbelief as in a rapt appreciation of technique. What this
technique might involve can be seen from a contemporary
account of Mrs Siddons's acting, praising her for what she did
not do rather than describing what she did. We are thus enabled
to imagine, in some measure, the more common style of the late
eighteenth century:

> No studied trick or start can be predicted; no forced tremulation of
> the figure, where the vacancy of the eye declares the absence of
> passion, can be seen; no laborious strainings at false climax, in which
> the tired voice reiterates one high note beyond which it cannot
> reach, is ever heard; no artificial heaving of the breasts, so disgusting
> when the affectation is perceptible; none of those arts by which the
> actress is seen, and not the character, can be found in Mrs. Siddons.
>
> Boaden: Memoirs 1.288–9

See now these extravagances transferred to literature in an
example from Jacques Cazotte's Le Diable amoureux, first
published in 1772:

> I then delivered the evocation in a distinct and resolute tone, and,
> swelling my voice, called out Belzebub! at three different times and at

very short intervals. I could feel a dreadful chillness run through my veins, and my hair stand on end. I had scarce spoken the word when from the top of the vault a double folded window flew open facing me, and I discovered a torrent of light which pierced through the aperture, and was more dazzling than the rays of the mid-day sun. The head of a camel of a dreadful shape and size appeared at the window. I was struck at the prodigious length of the animal's ears. The hideous monster opened its large mouth and roared out *Che vuoi?* (What do you want?) in a tone well suited to the rest of the apparition... all the neighbouring caves re-echoes with the tremendous *Che vuoi?*

This heightened sensibility, which to modern ears carries a touch of the ludicrous, should not be misunderstood. It was an essential component of the style of the period, rampant emotionalism dining elegantly upon a dish of horrors conveniently distanced by cold print or lithograph, and it depended for its full effect on the audience's recognizing convention when it saw or read it, in the manner of Greeks at a comedy by Menander, knowing which actor's mask represented which character and how one was supposed to react to his or her entrance on the scene. We can see the mechanics behind these exaggerations if we compare two versions of the same tale by Robert Burns. The first comes from a letter he wrote to an acquaintance, Francis Grose, in 1789 recounting the story of a farmer's meeting with witches:

Sir, Among the many Witch Stories I have heard relating to Alloway Kirk, I distinctly remember only two or three... [One market day, a farmer was returning home in the early hours of the morning when he saw a light coming from the church.] Though he was terrified with a blaze streaming from the kirk, yet as it is a well known fact, that to turn back on these occasions is running by far the greatest risk of mischief, he prudently advanced on his road. When he had reached the gate of the kirk-yard, he was surprised and entertained, through the ribs and arches of an old gothic window which still faces the highway, to see a dance of witches merrily footing it round their old sooty blackguard master, who was keeping them all alive with the power of his bagpipe. The farmer stopping his horse to observe them a little, could plainly descry the faces of many old women of his acquaintance and neighbourhood.

The tone is jaunty, the Devil portrayed without horror and the witches as peasants almost harmlessly engaged in a rustic round. In Burns's subsequent poem on the subject, *Tam o' Shanter* (1790), however, mere dancing is too tame and the reader is treated to a description of the dreadful objects which met Tam's sight as he fearfully peeped through a window into the church:

> Coffins stood round like open presses
>   [cupboards]
> That shaw'd the dead in their last dresses;
> And by some devilish cantraip slight [magical
>   trick]
> Each in its cauld hand held a light,
> By which heroic Tam was able
> To note upon the haly table
> A murderer's banes in gibbet airns [irons];
> Twa span-lang, wee, unchristen'd bairns;
> A thief, new cutted frae the rape
> Wi' his last gasp his gab did gape [still open-
>   mouthed] ...

A garter, which a babe had strangled;
A knife, a father's throat had mangled,
Whom his ain son o' life bereft,
The grey hairs yet stuck to the heft.

Self-conscious theatricality allied to equally self-conscious emotionalism, then, was a key-note of the period and should neither be forgotten nor discounted when it comes to consideration of the blossoming occultism which also marks the eighteenth and early nineteenth centuries. For this was the time of German Illuminism, French Martinism and Pasqually's theurgical Order of Elected Cohens, and Mesmerism, not to mention the immense proliferation of Masonic and pseudo-Masonic rites and Orders which were invented both to embody and satisfy the desire of the aristocrat and educated bourgeois for an esotericism free of conventional religion, but expressed through complex ritual in an atmosphere of secret (that is to say, exclusive) theatre. 'Rationality' was an ideal behaviour to which the educated of the period aspired. It scarcely began to inform their emotional or social existence.

With this in mind, it is worthwhile our looking briefly at the famous, and much over-used, paintings and drawing of witches by Goya. There were six altogether, produced in 1797-8 to hang in the Duchess of Osuna's boudoir in the family's country house. Two of the six are related to plays which satirize popular superstitions, and all have, and were intended to have, a bearing on the contrast between flattery of the 'rationalist' aristocracy on whose walls they were put on private show, and the 'superstitious' peasantry by whom the ducal property was surrounded and on whose labours it depended for its working. In the best-known of these, *The Witches' Sabbat* [plate 20], the appeal to what one might call delicious horror is evident not only in the grotesque form of Satan as a huge goat, but also in the details of the children who are being offered to him. One appears to be plump, almost fresh from the breast of his mother whose shoulder is being touched by the preternaturally long left arm of the goat; a second, however, is skeletal, although its pose clearly suggests it is alive, as it stretches out a long, thin left arm in mimickry of the goatish arm above it, and takes an eager, bony step in his direction. A third, equally skeletal, lies dead on the ground, ignored by the two women in front of it, one of whom carries three dead foetuses tied to a stick which rests casually on her left shoulder. (The device reminds one of Hogarth's *Gin Lane* (1751) in which a child is impaled on the spit of a dancing cook.) In the foreground lies the veiled figure of a woman with the fat legs of a child protruding from beneath her mantle. It is the merest hint of a Madonna, but sufficient to give the scene an extra thrill.

Contrast this piece of posed theatre, composed for a Duchess's private enjoyment, with the witches appearing in Goya's sequence of eighty prints entitled *Los Caprichos* (The Caprices), published in 1799. Their theme is contemporary Spain, their tone dark and deeply pessimistic. They were intended for public sale, and Goya himself advertised them in the *Madrid Daily*, using the terms 'ridicule' and 'fantasy' as part of his description of them. The Professor of Engraving at the Royal Academy in Madrid found them obscene.

Plate 19, *Allá vá eso*, illustrates Goya's view of the witches' flight. Two witches cling perilously to a broom as it flies through the air. One is hermaphroditic, apparently old, with a muscular torso and arms, slender legs, and small feet in comparison with the large hands. One hand grasps the broom handle, the other a hissing snake. Her/his face is turned upwards to look at a spitting cat, its back raised, its fur standing on end, as it holds the snake's tail in its claws. Behind the hermaphrodite crouches a young woman, her hair streaming behind her, her legs drawn right up under her body. She is looking down, although most of her face is obscured by the other witch's forearm. She appears to be borne along by an outstretched cape which has assumed the form of a bat's wings. It is difficult to tell whether the witches are rising from or descending to the open countryside spread out below them.

Again, this is drama, but of a completely different kind from that of the *Witches' Sabbat*. Here is no fantasy for a Duchess, but a moral comment on one of the key features of standard witch-craft theory: the Devil as the serpent of *Genesis*; the witch as an unnatural human being, female but not quite female, old as well as young; a hint of shape-changing; the presence of an attendant evil spirit; the indecency of the witches' nakedness; their preter-natural power derived from Satan – all threatening and looming large over a peaceful countryside from which they have come or which they may be about to infest. There is a seriousness about this drawing, which is absent from the *Witches' Sabbat* despite the horrors depicted therein, and the fact that it was produced for the general public suggests, perhaps, that Goya considered moral comment on a widespread, popular belief more important than the genteel shivers appropriate to the restricted circles of the aristocracy. The one was a response to the wishes of a particular patron, the other to a deep current in society at large.

One may also note, however, that Goya automatically links witchcraft with the countryside. It was an assumption (perhaps a hope?) common among the educated of the period. Thus, for example, we find James Crossley in the mid-nineteenth century writing of Pendle in his introduction to a re-issue of *Potts's Discoverie of Witches in the County of Lancaster*,

> The 'parting genius' of superstition still clings to the hoary hill tops and rugged slopes and mossy water sides, along which the old forest stretched its length, and the voices of ancestral tradition are still heard to speak from the depth of its quiet hollows, and along the course of its gurgling streams. He who visits Pendle will yet find that charms are generally resorted to among the lower orders...that each small hamlet has its peculiar and gifted personage whom it is dangerous to offend...that each locality has its haunted house; that apparitions still walk their ghostly rounds.

The tone is patronizing (although it was almost certainly not intended to be), and redolent of Romantic sentimentality which invested the countryside with burdens of nostalgia for a vanished past, which the real countryside was ill-equipped to bear. For Britain, perhaps England in particular, was being influenced by a desire which had originated in Germany, a desire for some kind of organic bond between nature and the prevalent culture and society itself, and out of these inchoate longings, allied to a very particular interpretation of the legacy of Greece and Rome, was born neo-paganism, less a movement, more a collective feeling among the educated elite that the grimy realism of the industrial revolution was less attractive, both physically and spiritually, than the natural purity and innate virtue of country life and manners.

When it came to expressing witchcraft in literature, however, Crossley's amicability was not the tone most likely to be heard. Avuncular toleration, indeed, would disappear in favour of the more dramatic association of witches with evil, and the description of a witch would revert very quickly to caricature in the style of a sixteenth-century woodcut. Compare, for example, plate 21 with the following portrait of a witch, taken from *The Wizard Priest and the Witch*, a novel in three volumes by Quintin Poynet, published in 1822:

Mother Wolfe was in person tall and erect, long-armed, squalid, gaunt, bony, and grim; the features of her face, the skin of which was furrowed with wrinkles and powdered thickly with sunburnt freckles and spots, were most repulsive and ill-favoured; her hazel eyes, which squinted with an expression of mischief, horrible and malignant, were overshadowed and overhung by a penthouse projection of low forehead, and a pair of huge grey, grizzled eyebrows, divers serpentine locks of the same colour and appearance hanging down on each side of her head and face, and giving her the semblance of the far-famed Gorgon of antiquity; her ill-shaped nose was disproportionably huge, and frightfully proboscous, overhanging a mouth of the very widest dimensions – so wide, indeed, that when opened to its extreme limits of expansion, the upper part of the head seemed for ever about to quit and relinquish its connection with the lower: this monstrous aperture was but indifferently furnished with teeth, and in some places the gums themselves had completely disappeared, and left exposed to view the aveolar process of the jaw; her chin was long and peaked, and woefully in want of some depilatory operation for the removal of the numerous hairs, both bristly and spiral, with which it was strewn. These defects of person, and ungraciousness of exterior, were, if possible, increased by the uncouthness and inelegance of her garb and coverings; her head being surmounted with a bonnet, similar to the head gear commonly ascribed to the celebrated Mother Shipton, and the rest of her frame wrapped closely in a sort of pelisse, or habit of the coarsest serge or cloth, in colour russet, darkened with dirt and smoke, and fastened securely round her waist by a band or belt of strong hempen cord.

Is there any cliché missing from this picture? Certainly the emphasis upon ugliness satisfies the eighteenth-century expectation of grotesquery in such subjects – even including the inappropriate but revealing reference to the 'inelegance' of her attire, a sure sign that the author was a middle-class writer accustomed to seeing and dealing with decently – even fashionably – dressed women, and thought 'inelegance' an unhappy mark of the lower classes. But the very completeness of the exaggeration indicates that we are here dealing with little more than a stage-character, a bogey-woman to frighten children, a mask in a comedy. So perhaps it is no accident that this is the portrait of the witch which continued its life as caricature in children's stories.

When it comes to a description of what witches were alleged to do, however, literature and reality come very much closer together. Take the maleficent magic attributed to a witch in a novel by Wilhelm Meinhold, *Sidonia the Sorceress*, published in 1847-8:

Now as the rumour of witchcraft spread through the village, all the people ran together, from every part, to Trina's house. And a pale young man pressed forward from amongst the crowd, to look at the supposed witch. When he stood before her, the girl cast down her eyes gloomily, and he cried out, 'It is she! it is the very accursed witch who robbed me of my strength by her sorceries, and barely escaped from the faggot – seize her – that is Anna Wolde.' Now he knew what the elder sticks meant, which he found set up as a gallows before his door this morning – the witch wanted to steal away his manhood from him again – burn her! burn her! Come and see the elder sticks, if they did not believe him!

So the whole village ran to his cottage, where he had just brought home a widow, whom he was going to marry, and there indeed stood the elder sticks right before his door in the form of a gallows, upon which the sheriff was wroth, and commanded the girl to be brought before him with her hands bound.

Objects intended to work or counteract malefice were still being found in the nineteenth and twentieth centuries. Witch bottles filled with thorns or pins or nails, and often topped up with urine, for example, were discovered concealed in a Somerset cottage in 1858, and four years earlier a workman cleaning out a pond in Yeovil dredged up a bottle containing three human figures stuck through with pins, with a sign of the planet Saturn attached to their breasts. Writing on the back of each doll made it clear that these were curse-figures, after the manner of Graeco-Roman *defixiones*, and there was even a piece of lead with magical engravings on it to complete the analogy. A somewhat more unpleasant instrument of malefice came to light in 1921 when customs officers in Naples confiscated an old woman's parcel and found it contained a lamb's head with forty-three nails driven into it, a discovery which immediately led to the woman's being identified as a witch and being attacked by a frightened crowd; and (lest it be thought that similar things do not happen everywhere), a case came before the Salisbury County Court in 1976 in which one neighbour was accused of attempting to work maleficent magic against another by sending him, via the post, a chicken's heart stuck with needles.

We may persuade ourselves, then, that a belief in the efficacy of magic and witchcraft did not die out during the eighteenth and nineteenth centuries, in spite of claims made by *bien pensants* who thought (and continue to think) of themselves as formers of public opinion. Not surprisingly, therefore, a note of uncertainty sometimes crept into their pronouncements:

> So low...is now the belief in witchcraft, that perhaps it is only received by those half-crazy individuals who feel a species of consequence derived from accidental coincidences, which, were they received by the community in general, would go near, as on former occasions, to cost the lives of those who make a boast of them. At least one hypochondriac patient is known to the author, who believes himself the victim of a gang of witches, and ascribes his illness to their charms, so that he wants nothing but an indulgent judge to awake again the old ideas of sorcery.
>
> Sir Walter Scott: *Letter on Demonology and Witchcraft*, 1830

Hoping that belief in witchcraft was now confined to the mentally ill, however, was a standard whistle in the dark for a century which also saw, for example, the rise of Spiritualism and Theosophy, the foundation of a kind of magical university in England (The Hermetic Order of the Golden Dawn), the growth of Spiritism in France, a movement which sought to reconcile supernatural beliefs with the latest scientific theories, and in Germany, a burgeoning fascination with poltergeists. Cunning folk, astrologers, fortune-tellers, witches – all continued to flourish, for there was no lack of clientele and nor was that clientele confined to what the nineteenth century regularly called 'the lower orders'. Society as a whole, in fact, continued to operate on more than one level simultaneously, as it always had done. The educated claimed to formulate orthodoxy for everyone else (and by 'orthodoxy' here, I mean the way people were expected to regard and explain the relationship between themselves and the rest of the universe), and as the educated controlled most of the means of disseminating information, sooner or later most people became aware of what that orthodoxy was supposed to be. In the Middle Ages, the formulator of opinion was the Catholic faith, and the means of dissemination were largely sermons, wall-paintings, and stained glass, with popular printed ballads and stories coming along in due time. In the early modern period the situation was essentially the same. By the nineteenth century, however, 'science' had become the new orthodoxy and a flood of cheap books, pamphlets, newspapers, and working men's lectures had become the principal means of its dissemination.

Yet in spite of the change in orthodoxy, people in general were always likely to behave as though the orthodoxy had not altered, and the laws of the magical universe still continued to operate. The problem for them, if indeed there was a problem, was that whereas in earlier times the magical viewpoint had blended in, often seamlessly, with the viewpoint of Christian orthodoxy, the new sciences would not easily allow such a blending. So society suffered another dislocation to add to those social upheavals it had suffered already. In the earlier period, the educated could criticize details of popular belief and practice, but essentially they and the general population accepted enough of the prevailing orthodoxy to maintain a whole world-view. God existed, Satan existed, angels and evil spirits existed, and interaction between these supernatural entities and human beings was not only possible, it actually did take place. In the eighteenth and nineteenth centuries, however, belief in Christianity in many intellectual circles was on the wane, and as they abandoned faith in God for faith in science, so the partnership between their world-view and that of the populace began to break down. Magic, depending as it does, on acknowledgement of a divine power at work in the universe, thus became isolated from the self-proclaiming opinion-makers in a way it had not done before. But because the opinion-makers had a grip on the dissemination of information, theirs gradually turned into the orthodoxy to which everyone at least paid lip service.

Cardinal Newman recognized the threat to religion, and, we should add, to magic and witchcraft as well:

> I do not shrink from uttering my firm conviction that it would be a gain to the country were it vastly more superstitious, more bigoted, more gloomy, more fierce in its religion than at present it shows itself to be... Rationalism is the great evil of the day.
>
> *Apologia Pro Vita Sua*, 1864

—◦ CHAPTER SIX ◦—

The Modern Witch

Conceptions of the witch do not disappear. They linger on well beyond the time of their greatest potency, and the image of the beautiful, young witch has never been forgotten in spite of the stereotype of the old, malevolent hag. Thus, when a nineteenth-century engraver was commissioned to illustrate Burns's poem, *Tam o' Shanter*, for example, he decided to present the reader with a single young female, scantily clad in a shift whose neckline is cut so low that it exposes both her breasts [plate 24]; and Otto Greiner (1869-1916) gives us a roomful of naked and semi-clad young witches – a study in female movement rather than a picture of evil cavortings: the scene could just as well be a turn-of-the-century brothel, apart from the horned skull nailed above the lintel.

A remarkable contrast in styles and intention can be seen, however, in two twentieth-century images. The first is a picture which was used for display in the Museum of Witchcraft in Bayonne. It displays a young, naked female rubbing herself with a magical unguent before flying to a Sabbat. She is surrounded by the trappings of mock-medievalism and a black cat rubs itself affectionately against her ankle. The effect of the whole is cosy, not to say twee, and not in the least threatening. There is no real suggestion that Satan might be in the background. This witch, despite the fact that she is apparently preparing to attend a diabolic convention at which, according to standard witch-theory, she would report on the evil she had done already and promise to do even worse in future before joining a demonic banquet and sexual orgy, should surely be of the so-called 'white' variety, her youth and her delicate pose acting as guarantees of her essentially beneficent nature. The second, however, a drawing from 1920 by the Austrian artist Alfred Kubin (1877-1959), is alto-gether different. Purporting to show a young witch in the process of magically changing shape, it depicts a distorted female figure, her startled eyes staring sideways at an open book containing the formula by which she has worked the mutation, her mouth open either in the act of recitation or in pain as the transformation begins to take effect. Her vagina gapes wide and prominent, while a snake starts to slither towards it. The brutal sexuality assaults the onlooker.

A combination of lasciviousness and the young, preferably naked female body inherited from the Classical tradition, then, is still able to co-exist with the cliché of the witch-as-crone. But the Christian tradition of the witch as a human being motivated by envy or hatred towards her (usually her) fellow creatures and covenanted in some way with the Devil has also lingered into modern times. An amalgam of these two can be found in the experience of Carole Compton, a twenty-year-old Scottish girl from Ayr who was working as a nanny on the island of Elba and arrested there on 2 August 1982 on charges of arson and attempted murder. Carole came to trial on 15 December 1983 and was found guilty of the charges relating to arson but dismissed on the charges of attempted murder on account of there being insufficient proof. What made the charges and the trial unusual was that, in effect, Carole was being accused of witchcraft, since it was alleged that the fires had been caused by Carole's casting the evil eye upon the household in general and upon the baby in her care in particular.

Carole had fallen in love with an Italian she had met in Ayr and followed him to Italy in May 1982 when he went back home, getting a job as a nanny before (so she hoped) they married and settled down. Curious incidents started to happen almost at once. In June, a little religious picture fell to the ground as she passed and was badly damaged. In July, the second floor of the house in which she was living with the family of her charge was burned to a ruin, and everyone was obliged to go to another apartment. Within the week, one of its rooms broke into flames, too. Politely, but firmly, the family declined to have Carole continue to live with them, so while they retired to Rome, Carole found a nannying job on Elba, moving there at the end of July.

She stayed in a house belonging to the grandparents of the three small children (one a baby), who were entrusted to her and immediately found that the grandmother did not like her. Within two days a fire was discovered in the grandparents' bedroom, and although no great harm was done on this occasion, a small statue in the living room inexplicably fell to the floor while Carole was present. The next day, other objects likewise fell – a cake stand, and a blue glass vase which broke. Now, for the first time, the grandmother openly used the word *strega*, 'witch', and said that Carole had the Devil on her back. Not long afterwards, on the very same day, fire broke out in the children's bedroom, and immediately the grandmother began to shriek that Carole had started the fires, that she was evil, and that she was a witch. Carole was therefore arrested, and the newspapers had their usual field day. A British newspaper, for example, published her photograph with the headline, 'The Girl they call a Witch', and an Italian magazine put her on its front cover with 'Strega' printed across it, and when Carole eventually came to trial in December the following year, an old woman tried to exorcize her by splashing her and her mother with holy water.

It is the details which make this case of particular interest. Carole was young and pretty, not the stereotype of a witch in either Italian or British folklore, and in fact that stereotype is less and less in evidence after the nineteenth and early twentieth centuries, confining itself to cartoons, some films, newspapers, and pantomime. Apart from these restricted media, where stereotypes are intended to hold sway, the twentieth century appears to prefer the youthful image, as two American television series, *Bewitched* and *Sabrina, the Teenage Witch*, seem to bear witness.

The scenes of Carole's alleged witchcraft were principally bedrooms and this is significant. For the bedroom is perhaps the most intimately familial room of the house, the area closed more than any other against the intrusion of strangers. Owen Davies (1999) has shown that as late as the twentieth century, visits even by a neighbour could be resented, and should they be frequently repeated in the face of discouragement, could be taken as evidence of attempted witchcraft. If entry into a living room or kitchen could provoke such reactions, how much more sensitive must be the bedroom where people are at their most vulnerable and so most open to invasive harm. Not for nothing is the bedroom the place physically entered by witches, as we read in many an indictment at their trials, or spiritually assaulted when they appear in waking dreams, either in their own shape or in those of lights or animals. It is not surprising, therefore, that Carole's maleficent magic should be seen as particularly intrusive and dangerous, especially for the children.

Carole's accusers were of the opinion that her magical effects were the result of her evil eye. Here we have a complex phenomenon which is susceptible of a number of different explanations by those who live with it or have had occasion to suffer from it. Some of these are relevant to Carole's situation. For example, the evil eye may appear to work in the midst of strained social relations where at least one of the offended parties is afraid that a particular cultural system or social boundary is under threat. Carole was resented from the first by the grandmother who openly wondered why a foreigner had been employed to look after her grandchildren. The evil eye may offer an explanation for deviant happenings, in Carole's case such as a picture, a statue, or a vase falling to the floor for no apparent reason. Carole herself was puzzled by one or two of these phenomena and could not explain them, and neither could anyone else in spite of attempts to suggest that both the falling objects and the outbreaks of fire could have been caused by group-generated recurrent spontaneous psychokinesis, a suggestion which did not really satisfy anyone. This ignorance on Carole's part, however, is interesting because the evil eye has been described as 'a form of witchcraft in which the bewitching person may not be aware of his own power and may have no evil intent'.[1] In connection with this, it would also be instructive to know what was the colour of Carole's eyes, or whether she was menstruating during the key days on which her supposed witchcraft was most evident, since these might be factors influencing the hostile reaction she received from the family, factors whose importance she might well not have realized or even thought about.

Finally, it may be noted that popular newspapers and magazines were happy to print and 'investigate' her story. They took the expected line that the allegation of witchcraft was nonsense, and made much of peasant superstition – either not knowing or not caring that one of the principals in Carole's story was actually a young, city-dwelling businesswoman – but were confident enough that the very mention of witchcraft would be sufficient to intrigue their readers and capture their interest. Witchcraft, it seems, still has the power to attract an audience. This may be in part because in the West the subject has now reached the stage of being exotic, a manifestation of colourful strangeness in a society largely secular and materialist. But the word 'witch' has also undergone something of a change in its associations, and since the birth and growth of modern pagan witchcraft, more usually known as 'Wicca', one cannot be quite sure what the word will convey to those who hear or read it.

Wicca arose from a stream fed by a number of different rivulets from the eighteenth and nineteenth centuries, which have been described in detail by Ronald Hutton (1999): (i) ancient paganism which was seen as a dark, violent force by whose compulsion idolaters had offered blood sacrifices to savage divinities; (ii) a dignified Graeco-Roman inheritance which, it was hoped, would enable the present to keep at bay the disturbing aspects of paganism and assist in the constant progression of modern society onwards and upwards; (iii) the fusion of modern science and Eastern mysticism created by Madame Blavatsky to form a new system of philosophical and spiritual endeavour known as Theosophy; and (iv) neo-paganism which sprang from late eighteenth-century German Romanticism and laid great stress on a joyous, liberating, non-Christian force it called 'Nature'. Together these suggested a fresh approach towards religion, one which rejected traditional Christianity, deified (or at least heroized) Nature, and claimed that a spark of divinity is immanent in every human being.

But Wicca needed an inventor or discoverer, and it seems clear that this role was filled by Gerald Gardner (1884-1964). Gardner had come to witchcraft via other occult interests which included membership of a group which worked quasi-Masonic and Pythagorean rituals and, for one year only, opened a theatre with a view to presenting mysticism to the general public through the medium of drama. Gardner also belonged to the *Ordo Templi Orientis* (The Order of the Eastern Temple) which offered candidates an amalgam of mystical Freemasonry, a nineteenth-century version of magic, and Indian tantra and yoga, in a framework of myth relating to the Knights Templar as the supposed keepers of a particular system of arcane knowledge. Then in September 1939, according to his version of events, he was initiated into witchcraft by a woman called Dorothy Clutterbuck, high priestess of a non-Christian religion which had survived from ancient times into modern. This Dorothy, however, is unlikely to have been quite as Gardner described her, and was probably a respectable private tutor of music and elocution – the driving force behind the Rosicrucian Theatre of which Gardner, as I said, was a member – and his partner in an enterprise which 'reconstructed' a sixteenth-century witch's cottage, the original of the Clutterbuck dwelling-place. Not that Gardner's version was entirely fiction. This theatre-set cottage actually did provide a suitable, atmospheric meeting-place for a coven of modern witches, led by the real Dorothy (or 'Dafo' as Gardner used to call her) and Gardner himself during the early 1950s.

The question at this point, however, is what did Gardner and his contemporaries understand by 'witches' and 'witchcraft'? For that we have to look back a few decades. Charles Leland (1824–1903), an American folklorist, claimed to have met an hereditary witch during one of his visits to Italy. They struck up a friendship and 'Maddalena' introduced him to other witches who entrusted him with many of the secrets of their craft or religion. From this experience stemmed a number of books among which *Aradia, or The Gospel of the Witches*, published in 1889, is the best-known. *Aradia* purports to be the transcription of a traditional witch legend, but was probably a concoction by Leland himself, although opinion is divided on this point. It contains an assertion which was to make a great impact on later witchcraft studies. The victims of the early modern persecution of witches, it said, were in fact noble-souled rebels against feudalism, and this romantic notion was taken up and fuelled by subsequent writers (mainly English), until in 1921 an Egyptologist, Margaret Murray (1862–1963), published the first of two books presenting a novel theory of witchcraft to English readers.

The Witch Cult in Western Europe suggested that up to the seventeenth century there had been a fertility cult in continuous existence, worshipping a horned god and meeting in groups of thirteen, each coven being linked with others in a web of organization. Covens met four times a year. Their meetings, which Murray called 'esbats', provided feasting, dancing, magical ceremonies, sacrifices of animals and children, and ritual copulation. The members of these covens were, of course, the witches and their persecution during the early modern period was an attempt by the official ecclesiastical authorities to stamp out these last remnants of the 'old religion'. This account was followed in 1933 by *The God of the Witches*, purporting to trace the origin and survival of the horned god in European history and folklore. Now, despite efforts by some people to show that Murray knew what she was talking about, the fact is that her theory is complete nonsense, based upon poor scholarship, wishful thinking, and deliberate omission of any evidence which did not support her thesis. Demolition has been done more than once and is irrefutable. Nevertheless, the 1940s saw sales of her books suddenly rocket, and the myth that female witches – the male variety is scarcely heeded in this version of history – were slaughtered in vast numbers, yet still managed to survive and preserve a non-patriarchal religion, has proved popular and very influential. Even her unsustainable fiction that a coven consisted of thirteen people has entered public consciousness as a fact.

Now, Gardner both knew and approved of her books, since he used a number of their ideas in his novel *High Magic's Aid* (1949) and in his first non-fiction work on the subject, *Witchcraft Today*, published in 1954. At some point between these two, he had established a coven in Hertfordshire which performed seasonal fertility rituals, danced in the nude – Gardner was quite keen on naturism – and invoked spirits for beneficent magical purposes, the key features now associated with modern pagan witchcraft. The rituals he employed came largely from the *Book of Shadows*, a compilation of beliefs, rituals, incantations, magical instructions, and various other aspects of the witch's craft necessary or useful for the guidance of an individual witch or a coven. There is actually no definitive version of this book, since modern witch-craft is nothing if not individualistic, and indeed its format changed during Gardner's own lifetime as his most famous initiate, Doreen Valiente, altered, excised, and added to the material with his approval.

The Wicca Gardner created (perhaps it would be better and more accurate to say set in motion), was thus a form of neo-pagan religion with its own distinctive beliefs and philosophy which have now out-lived and outgrown their originator. Wiccans – although this is not a title which would be altogether acceptable to many modern witches – tend to be pantheists and polytheists, while using a named male (the Horned God) and female divinity (the Goddess) in their rituals, the latter usually exercising supremacy over the former. Nature is honoured, the instruction that no living thing should be harmed is a guiding principle, worship is often performed in the nude, and magic of various kinds is operated, all with the intention of promoting the welfare of individuals or groups or the earth itself. Gardner's interest in the sexual aspects of tantric magic, which he would have met during his membership of the *Ordo Templi Orientis*, led him to include copulation as one of the magical rites of his tradition, although the act may be symbolic as well as actual. Ritual scourging was also encouraged as a means of purification of suffering, and the main ceremonies were supposed to take place on those festivals which had been described by Margaret Murray.

Wicca, however, is a very fluid system and the form in which Gardner organized it not only changed itself but quickly gave rise to others. Indeed, since each coven is meant to be autonomous there can be no centralizing authority to impose a single theology or set of rituals on anyone practising witchcraft; therefore change is an integral part of the whole religion. Thus the Gardnerian tradition, for example, was challenged during the 1960s by Alexander and Maxine Sanders. Alexander (1926-1988) claimed he had been initiated into Wicca by his grandmother, after which he learned and practised a variety of different forms of magic. By 1966 he and his wife had become the best-known witches in Britain, largely because they actively courted publicity and were accorded it in full measure. It was a time, of course, when hippies and the New Age gallimaufry of beliefs and philosophies were creating public interest and, to some extent, a favourable atmosphere for the exotic and flamboyant. Basing their practice of witchcraft on Gardner's *Book of Shadows*, the Sanders nevertheless deviated from it in a number of significant ways. Following Alexander's particular interest, they employed a ritual magic derived from the Hermetic magic of the Renaissance and mediated via the nineteenth-century occultist, Eliphas Levi. They also emphasized the importance of astral projection, clairvoyance, and the use of charms and talismans. Alexander was, or maintained he was, favourably inclined to orthodox Christians (although how orthodox Christians could have expressed any approval of what he was doing is not explained), and at one point is even credited with saying that being a good witch would help someone to be a better Christian. But the only real point of contact he had with Christianity – and even this was tenuous – was to see the world in Manichaean terms as an occult battleground between good and evil.

The Gardnerian and Alexandrian traditions may be the best-known in Wicca, but the highly individualistic nature of modern witchcraft means that they are actually no more than two among many. 'Dianic' witches, for example, are strongly feminist and worship the Goddess more or less exclusively. Female power is the one emphasized in this tradition, and its members tend to be active politically as well as magically. 'Hereditary' and 'Traditional' covens claim to pre-date Gardner and are led by a priest rather than a priestess. They work clothed and are careful to distinguish themselves in the details of their ritual practices from what is generally known as 'Wicca'. Other, even more modern traditions include 'Fairy', 'Celtic', 'Seax-Wica', and 'Witchcraft as a Science', each placing its particular emphasis in accordance with what its title may suggest. Individual witches belonging to no established coven are also numerous:

> Moon Raven is a solitary practitioner of eclectic Earth Spirituality practices. Her Spirituality emphasizes Irish Wicca (Witta), but draws from many other areas of spirituality, including shamanism and Native American.
>
> http://www.amysticalgrove.com/BOS/

This eclecticism is a common feature of the forms of modern witchcraft practised by individuals. It could scarcely be otherwise, given the freedom, for example, which witches enjoy to create their own rituals and approach the divine in creation. Moreover, the rapid growth of the global flow of information means that a witch is not restricted to the printed word – however diverse the books she or he may consult for inspiration. The huge variety of available television channels allows instant access to living folklore, magical ceremonies, healing rituals, shamanic rites, from all over the world, while the constant multiplication of websites on the Internet enables the witch to enrich her or his own imaginative devices with the imaginations and experiences of countless other practitioners.

In fact, however, there are really two forms of witchcraft operating in the modern West. One may be described, perhaps, as a continuity from earlier times in that its practitioners work magic in ways and for purposes which would have been familiar to their predecessors in the early modern period. The other has emerged from and is a continuing development of the pagan witchcraft which belongs essentially to the nineteenth and twentieth centuries, its main aim being directed towards the formation of an intimate connection between the witch and the world around her or him. Margot Adler, one of the best known of the modern American witches, provides a magical exercise which illustrates the point:

> Perhaps the best way to begin to understand the power behind the simple word *witch* is to enter the circle... Do it, perhaps, on a full moon, in a park, or in the clearing of a wood. You don't need any of the tools you will read about in books on the Craft. You need no special clothes or lack of them. Perhaps you might make up a chant, a string of names of gods and goddesses who were loved or familiar to you from childhood myths, a simple string of names for earth and moon and stars, easily repeatable like a mantra.
>
> And perhaps, as you say those familiar names and feel the earth and the air, the moon appears a bit closer, and perhaps the wind rustling the leaves suddenly seems in rhythm with your own breathing. Or perhaps the chant seems louder and all the other sounds far away. Or perhaps the woods seem strangely noisy. Or unspeakably still. And perhaps the clear line that separates you from the bird and tree and small lizards seems to melt. Whatever else, your relationship to the world of living nature changes. The Witch is the change of definitions and relationships.
>
> *Drawing Down the Moon* (Boston, Beacon 1971), 43-4

Here, clearly expressed, is the witch as an instrument in the process of what has been called *re-ligio*, a 're-linking' of the individual with the divine source of being, humanity with nature, matter with spirit, and other disjuncted pairs which the Creator intended to co-exist in harmony, an ecological spirituality involving both a transformation and an empowerment of the self, and it is this emphasis upon the interactive experience of the individual, and the belief that the way in which a person becomes a magical being is as important to the modern practice of magic as the goal of any specific magical operation, which marks perhaps more than anything else a difference in outlook between modern practitioners of magic and witchcraft and those of the earlier periods.

This tendency to introversion and the desire for a restoration of broken links with all parts of Nature can be illustrated by some of the results of an occult census of Britain carried and published by the *Sorcerer's Apprentice* in Leeds in 1989. In answer to the question – does occultism help/enhance one's social life? – positive replies thought that it imparted community spirit among like-minded people, made one aware of other people's feelings, gave a balanced view of life, gave one methods to help others, and developed a sense of spirituality behind everything. Not for nothing were the Greens the first choice of preferred political party among responding occultists. Empathy with nature is, as we have seen, a distinctive feature of much modern magic, and of modern witchcraft in particular. Who were these respondents? The majority had careers requiring at least a fairly high standard of education: nursing, engineering, computer programming, journalism, the Civil Service. Most were young. The average age of those in the census sample was 32, with 43.6% of that total in the age range 20–29, and a further 25.74% aged between 30 and 39. Most were male (62%). This, however, may be a reflection of the wide range of occult interests covered by the census, and one must remember that modern witchcraft, far from being predominantly female, often encourages an equal number of males and females in its workings in order to preserve a desirable balance of energies.

The older forms of magic seem to have been far less solipsistic. Hermetic, or learned magic, it is true, tended to concentrate on the relationship between the operator and God, or between the operator and higher, spiritual entities who formed with him a part of creation but existed within spheres more elevated and therefore less material than that of earth. But this type of magic was not witchcraft. Witchcraft, to return to the circular definition I mentioned earlier in the book, is what witches do, and what witches have done from the earliest times to the present constitutes a practical magic for good or bad intentions. It is this type of operation, geared to a discernible outcome rather than being part of a personal transformative process, which most clearly represents the continuous tradition and is distinct from its modern pagan counterpart.

That it is continuous can easily be demonstrated. The periodical *Newsweek*, for example, noted on 21 July 1997 that witchcraft has survived Communism in the Soviet Union and is emerging in post-Communist Russia, Belarus, and the Ukraine with ever-increasing popularity. People consult their local witch for precisely the same reasons as their ancestors did: to seek a cure for cattle fever, an antidote to childhood illnesses, or the death of a business rival. Practising witchcraft may also turn out to be as dangerous as ever it was; for it has been reported that four witches were killed by burning and two beaten to death in Siberia and northern Russia between 1993 and 1997.

But if we want evidence of continuity, which will help to throw light on the earlier historical periods, perhaps the most useful investigation of Western witchcraft in a modern setting is that carried out between 1969 and 1971 in the Bocage of Mayenne by the French anthropologist, Jeanne Favret-Saada. She has this to say about what she calls 'an attack of witchcraft':

A set of words spoken in a crisis situation by someone who will later be designated as a witch is afterwards interpreted as having taken effect on the body and belongings of the person spoken to, who will on that ground say he is bewitched.

Deadly Words, 9

This insistence upon *words*, whether or not accompanied by gestures, is important for understanding medieval and early modern expectations of and reactions to magic, for it is by means of the power of words that preternatural effects were achieved or, if you like, believed to be achieved. Hence we often read that a witch retired from a situation (perhaps confrontational, perhaps not) 'muttering', and it was the fact of this muttering which led to the accuser's assumption that magic had been set in motion. 'Witchcraft,' as Favret-Saada says, 'is spoken words,' and 'these spoken words are power, and not knowledge or information'. Talking about acts of witchcraft is therefore not as simple as it looks, for the complainer or accuser is not merely passing on information about a magical situation he or she wants resolved. In consulting an unwitcher, for example, the complainer is actively seeking to counteract that magic by which he or she has been caught. The words of complaint, the description of what he or she is suffering, are part of the verbal process whereby the witch will be identified and disempowered. So much is clear from the records and from Favret-Saada's description of modern unwitchers in the Bocage.

But we must bear in mind that when someone went to the authorities, ecclesiastical or lay, in earlier times and laid a charge of witchcraft against an individual, that process of complaining was no different from going to an unwitcher. The complainer, in fact, had simply chosen an 'official' as opposed to an unofficial

type of unwitcher, quite possibly on the grounds that the unofficial unwitcher had either been ineffectual in resolving the
situation, or was not considered to have sufficient power to be
able to produce a satisfactory resolution. This may help to explain
why many years, often decades, went by before someone was
denounced to the authorities as a witch. It is true, of course, that
witches were regularly used by members of their communities
who wished to benefit from their magical powers, but the
presence of a hostile magical practitioner in the community for
years on end without denunciation cannot be explained simply
by a presumed climate of fear surrounding her or his person. It
is a question of not talking in order to avoid a repetition of a
bewitchment which has already happened. Talking about it,
admitting that one has been bewitched, is an admission that one
is weaker than the witch, and such an admission provides an open
invitation to her, or to anyone else who may have the ability or
desire to exercise preternatural power against one, to use that
same magical power to one's ultimate disadvantage. Even the
acknowledgement that one has been helped rather than damaged
by magical means is an admission of weakness relative to the
magical operator. Hence silence is not so much a reaction of fear
as a sensible precautionary measure.

So complaining about a person's magical activity, even simply
designating someone as a witch, either by means of a complaint
to the authorities or as an unguarded, provocatory exclamation
in the heat of a quarrel with that individual, is in itself a magical
act, since it happened as the result of a decision (deliberate or
spontaneous) to go on the attack. Favret-Saada expresses it
starkly: 'No one escapes violence: he who does not attack automatically becomes the victim'. Hence, when individuals were
arrested and accused of practising witchcraft, they might well

deny it. Once again, however, simple fear of the consequence of their admitting the truth of the accusation is not quite enough to explain the denial. If a former victim has found the strength to put his or her situation into words and has thereby allied him or herself with the spiritual and physical powers of the Church or the magistracy, a reversal of roles has taken place. The accused witch has now been put in the position of weakness relative to the former victim, and only silence will afford some measure of protection from this attack by disengaging the individual from what is, in effect, a magical conversation. For talking about magic is, to one extent or another, to engage in it.

Let us therefore draw two conclusions from the foregoing. First, the traditional or historic witchcraft I have just been discussing has little in common with modern pagan witchcraft; and secondly, the presence of both types in modern Western society gives the lie to those romantics who, ever since the eighteenth century, have imagined that increasing education and the advance of the sciences were bound to put an end to centuries of 'foolish superstition'.

Two examples will suffice. First, in 1986, a survey in West Germany found that 33% of those questioned expressed a firm belief in the reality of witchcraft. Secondly, on 1 December 1950, Lieutenant-Commander R.H. Thompson stood up in the House of Commons in Westminster in support of the Fraudulent Mediums Bill which proposed to put right abuses arising from the Witchcraft Act of 1735 and the Vagrancy Act of 1824. The Bill had been put forward at least in part because of the well-known case of Helen Duncan, a Scottish medium, who in 1944 had been found guilty of intention to defraud the public, under the terms of the 1735 Act, and gaoled for nine months. The new Bill therefore concerned itself largely with Spiritualism and the effect which a repeat of the two Acts might have on those who genuinely believed they were able, in some way or another, to contact the spirits of the dead. Commander Thompson expressed himself as follows on the subject:

> In 1735 the Witchcraft Act brought to an end officially what had, in fact, been at an end for some years – the belief in the reality of witch-craft. Witchcraft had been practised from the very beginning of time; during the 16th and 17th centuries there was tremendous activity in England and on the Continent, but with the dawn of the 'age of reason' so called, belief in the reality of witchcraft faded.

To this, the MP for Clapham added his own piece of wishful thinking:

> I think it is right that all men and women should be free to express their own personal points of view, whatever those may be ... The answer to the false philosophies which, in our view, they may have developed, is not to make it illegal for people to express them, but to preach a better philosophy. The real cure of the things with which the Witchcraft Act attempted to deal is to extend complete education and knowledge in wider and wider circles.

But reality, as we have seen, turned out otherwise. So much for the pious hopes of *philosophes* and libertarians.

NOTES

'Witches' in Greece and Rome

1 *Naturalis Historia* 30.1
2 Dio Cassius 49.43.5
3 Livy 39.41.5-6; 40.43.3
4 Pindar: *Pythian* 4.214-17. Cf.
　　Horace: *Epodes* 17.6-7;
　　Anthologia Graeca 5.205
5 Antiphon 1.14-20
6 *Amores* 3.7.270-30
7 23
8 29
9 36
10 59, 48
11 31
12 51
13 91
14 101
15 129
16 7.17
17 *Philosophical Fragments*, 19
18 *Moralia* 680d
19 Pliny: *NH* 38.39
20 Plutarch: *Moralia* 414e
21 *Persae* 619-80
22 Cicero: *In Vatinium* 14; Tertullian:
　　Apologeticus 1.23.1

23 Suetonius: *Nero* 34.40
24 VIII.1b and 8a-b
25 Pliny: *NH* 18.41-2
26 Tacitus: *Annals* 2.69
27 *Symposium* 202e-203a
28 *De Iside et Osiride* 360d-e
29 Aristotle: *Athenian Constitution*
　　57.3
30 Iamblichus: *De mysteriis* 10.6
31 210-392
32 16.172
33 5.47; *Iliad* 24.343
34 *Argonautica* 4.1665-72
35 *Bellum Civile* 6.461-3
36 509
37 557-8
38 *De natura deorum* 1.43
39 *De divinatione* 2.148
40 *Elegies* 4.5.13-18
41 *Amores* 1.8.13-14
42 *De divinatione* 1.65
43 Horace: *Odes* 1.27.21-2
44 Ovid: *Amores* 3.7.29
45 Martial 11.49 50 .8
46 Apuleius: *Metamorphoses* 1.8-11

Enter the Christian Witch

1 *Clementine Recognitions* 4.14-15
2 *De civitate Dei* 10.11
3 *De doctrina Christiana* 2.20.30

4 *Contra Celsum* 1.60
5 *De caelesti hierarchia* 7-9
6 *Apologia pro Christianis*, 24

7   3.297

8   *Anthologia Graeca* 11.427

9   *On envy* 4

10   *Moralia* 680f–681a

11   Aquinas: *Summa Theologiae*
     1a.117.art.3. ad.2

12   3.16.1; 9.16.1–12; 9.38.3–4, 6–8;
     9.40.1; 9.42.2,4; 11.36.7;
     16.5.34

13   29.1.29–32

14   26.3.3

15   28.1.14

16   29.2.25

17   29.2.28

18   *Lex Romana Raetica Curiensis*
     Book 9, no. 13

19   *MGH Leges* 5.164

20   Nos. 197, 376, 198

21   *MGH Leges* 2. i. 222–4

22   Elvira 305

23   Venice 465, Rome 494

24   Seligenstadt 1012

25   Agda 506, Orléans 511, Auxerre 578

26   Braga 560–5, Narbonne 589,
     Clovesho 747

27   Braga 560–5

28   Seligenstadt 1012

29   Auxerre 578, Braga 675

30   Toledo 683

31   Toledo 694

32   Mainz 813, Aachen 836

33   Book 3, chapter 17

34   *Corrector*, chapter 5

35   *Polycraticus* 2.17

36   *Quaestio de strigis*

37   *De bono universali* Book 2,
     chapter 56

38   Book 2, chapter 4

A Plague of Witches

1   *Malleus* Part 1, question 18

2   Part 3, question 13

3   *De potestate Papae*, Chapter 12

4   *Universae Theologiae Systema*, arti-
     cle 8, questions 14 and 15

5   *Extirpacion de la Idolatria del Piru*,
     chapter 6

Trying a Witch

1   Book 5, chapter 12

Neither Gone Nor Forgotten

1   *Dictionnaire Philosophique*

2   *Avis au public sur les parricides
     imputés aux Calas et aux
     Sirven*, 1766

The Modern Witch

1   Blum & Blum, 154

Meyer M. & Mirecki P. (edd.): *Ancient Magic and Ritual Power* (Brill, Leiden 1995)

Meyer M. & Smith R. (edd.): *Ancient Christian Magic: Coptic Texts of Ritual Power* (Harper SanFrancisco 1994)

Pagels E.: *The Origin of Satan* (Allen Lane, Penguin 1996)

Reeves M.: *The Influence of Prophecy in the later Middle Ages* (Clarendon, Oxford 1969)

Russell J.B.: *Lucifer: the Devil in the Middle Ages* (Cornell University Press 1984)

Salmón F. & Cabré M.: 'Fascinating women: the evil eye in medical Scholasticism', in R. Frech, J. Arizzabalaga, A. Cunningham, L. García-Ballester (eds.): *Medicine from the Black Death to the French Disease* (Ashgate 1998), 53–84

Smith M.: *Jesus the Magician* (London, Victor Gollancz 1978)

Vikan G.: 'Art, medicine and magic in early Byzantium', *Dumbarton Oaks Papers* 38 (1984), 65–86

Vliet J. van der: 'Satan's fall in Coptic magic', in Meyer & Mirecki (edd.): *Ancient Magic and Ritual Power* q.v. 401–418

A Plague of Witches

Anglo S.: 'Evident authority and authoritative evidence: the Malleus Maleficarum', in S. Anglo (ed.): *The Damn'd Art* (Routledge & Kegan Paul, London 1977)

Ankarloo B.: 'Magies scandinaves et sorciers du nord', in R. Muchembled (ed.): *Magie et sorcellerie en Europe* q.v. 195–213

—: 'Sweden, the mass burnings (1668-1676)', in B. Ankarloo & G. Henningsen (edd.): *Early Modern European Witchcraft* q.v. 285–317

Ankarloo B. & Henningsen G. (edd.): *Early Modern European Witchcraft*, (Clarendon, Oxford 1990)

Bartlett R.: *Trial by Fire and Water: The Mediaeval Judicial Ordeal* (Oxford, Clarendon 1986)

Bechtel G.: *La sorcière et l'Occident* (Plon, Paris 1997)

Behar R.: 'Sexual witchcraft, colonialism, and women's powers: views from the Mexican Inquisition', in A. Lavrin (ed.): *Sexuality and Marriage in Colonial Latin America* (University of Nebraska Press 1989), 178–206

Behringer W.: 'Allemagne, 'mère de tant de sorcières, au coeur des persécutions', in R. Muchembled (ed.): *Magie et sorcellerie en Europe* q.v. 59–98

—: *Shaman of Obertsdorf: Chonrad Stoecklin and the Phantoms of the Night*, English translation (University Press of Virginia 1998)

—: *Witchcraft Persecutions in Bavaria*, English translation, (Cambridge University Press 1997)

Bever E.: 'Old age and witchcraft in early modern Europe', in P. Stearns (ed.): *Old Age in Preindustrial Society* (New York 1982), 150–190

—: 'Witchcraft fears and psychosocial factors in disease', *Journal of*

Interdisciplinary History 30 (Spring 2000), 573-590

Boyer P. & Nissenbaum S.: *Salem Possessed* (Harvard University Press 1974)

Brann N.L.: *Trithemius and Magical Theology* (State University of New York 1999)

Breslaw E.G.: *Tituba, Reluctant Witch of Salem* (New York University Press 1996)

Cassar C.: *Witchcraft, Sorcery, and the Inquisition* (Mireva, Malta 1996)

—: *Sex, Magic, and the Periwinkle: A Trial at the Malta Inquisition Tribunal, 1617* (Malta 2000)

Cave T.: *Pré-histoires: textes troublés au seuil de la modernité* (Droz, Geneva 1999)

Cervantes F.: *The Devil in the New World: The Impact of Diabolism in New Spain* (Yale University Press 1994)

Clark S.: *Thinking With Demons* (Clarendon, Oxford 1999)

Gentilcore D.: *From Bishop to Witch: The System of the Sacred in Early Modern Terra d'Otranto* (Manchester University Press 1992)

Godbeer R.: *The Devil's Dominion: Magic and Religion in Early New England*, (Cambridge University Press 1992)

Gruzinski S.: *The Conquest of Mexico* (Polity Press 1993)

Haliczer S.: *Inquisition and Society in the Kingdom of Valencia* (Berkeley, Los Angeles 1990)

Hall D.D.: *Witch-Hunting in Seventeenth-Century New England*, (Northeastern University Press, Boston 1991)

Heinemann E.: *Witches: A Psychoanalytical Exploration of the Killing of Women* (London 2000)

Henninsen G.: 'Witch hunting in Denmark', *Folklore* 93 (1982), 131-137

Higgs Strickland D.: 'Monsters and Christian enemies', *History Today*, (February 2000), 45-51

Hill F.: *A Delusion of Satan* (Hamish Hamilton, London 1996)

Hirsch P.: *The Printed Word and Its Diffusion* (Variorum Reprints, London 1978), no. XVI

Hodgen M.T.: *Early Anthropology in the Sixteenth and Seventeenth Centuries*, (University of Pennsylvania Press 1964)

Hoffer P.C.: *The Devil's Disciples: Makers of the Salem Witchcraft Trials* (John Hopkins University Press 1996)

—: *The Salem Witchcraft Trials: A Legal History* (University of Kansas 1997)

Houdard S.: *Les sciences du diable: quatre discours sur la sorcellerie* (Cerf, Paris 1992)

Jacques-Chaquin N. & Préaud M. (edd.): *Le sabbat des sorciers en Europe, xve-xviiie siècles* (Jérôme Millon, Grenoble 1993)

Johansen J.C.V.: 'Denmark, the sociology of accusations', in B. Ankarloo & G. Henningsen (edd.): *Early Modern European Witchcraft* q.v. 339-365

Jakobsen M.D.: *Shamanism* (Berghahn Books 1999)

Kieckhefer R.: *European Witch Trials* (Routledge & Kegan Paul, London 1976)

Langbein J.H.: *Prosecuting Crime in the Renaissance* (Harvard University Press 1974)

—: *Torture and the Law of Proof* (University of Chicago 1977)

Larner C.: 'Crimen exceptum? The crime of witchcraft in Europe', in V.A.C.
Gatrell, B. Lenman, G. Parker (edd.): *Crime and the Law*, (London 1980),
49-75

McGinn B.: *Antichrist* (Harper SanFrancisco 1994)

Martin R.: *Witchcraft and the Inquisition in Venice, 1550-1650* (Oxford University
Press 1989)

Maxwell-Stuart P.G.: (ed.): *Martín del Rio, Investigations into Magic*, (Manchester
University Press 2000)

—*Satan's Conspiracy: Magic and Witchcraft in Sixteenth-Century Scotland* (Tuckwell
Press 2000)

—: *Witchcraft in Europe and the New World, 1400-1800*, (Palgrave, London 2000)

Meurger M.: 'Plantes à illusion: l'interprétation pharmacologique du sabbat', in
N. Jacques-Chaquin & M. Préaud (edd.): *Le sabbat des sorciers* q.v. 369-382

Muchembled R. (ed.): *Magie et sorcellerie en Europe du Moyen Age à nos jours*
(Armand Colin, Paris 1994)

Pearl J.L.: *The Crime of Crimes: Demonology and Politics in France, 1560-1620*,
(Wilfred Laurier University Press 1999)

Peters E.: *The Magician, the Witch, and the Law* (University of Pennsylvania 1978)

Roper L.: *Oedipus and the Devil* (Routledge 1994)

Rosenthal B.: *Salem Story: Reading the Witch Trials of 1692* (Cambridge
University Press 1993)

Sánchez Ortega M.H.: 'Sorcery and eroticism in love magic', in M.E. Perry
& A.J. Cruz (edd.): *Cultural Encounters*, (University of California 1991),
58-92

Snow D.R.: *The Iroquois* (Blackwell, Oxford 1994)

Sörlin P.: *Wicked Arts: Witchcraft and Magic Trials in Southern Sweden, 1635-1754*
(Brill, Leiden 1999)

Tausiet Carlés M.: 'Le sabbat dans les traités espagnols sur la superstition et la
sorcellerie aux xvie et xviie siècles', in N. Jacques-Chaquin & M. Préaud
(edd.): *Le sabbat des sorciers* q.v. 259-279

Tedeschi J.: 'Inquisitorial law and the witch', in B. Ankarloo & G. Henningsen
(edd.): *Early Modern European Witchcraft* q.v. 83-118

—: 'The Roman Inquisition and witchcraft: an early seventeenth century
"Instruction" on correct trial procedure', *Revue de l'histoire des Religions* 200
(1983), 163-188

Trigger B.G.: *Natives and Newcomers: Canada's 'Heroic Age' Reconsidered*,
(Manchester University Press 1986)

—: *The Huron, Farmers of the North* (Holt-Rinehart-Winston 1969)

Vecsey C.: *Traditional Ojibwa Religion and its Historical Changes* (American
Philosophical Society, Philadelphia 1983)

Waardt H. de: 'Chasing demons and curing mortals: the medical practice of
clerics in the Netherlands', in H. Marland & M. Pelling (edd.): *The Task of
Healing* (Erasmus, Rotterdam 1996), 171-203

Walinski-Kiehl R.: 'La chasse aux sorcières et le sabbat des sorcières dans les évêchés de Bamberg et Würzburg (vers 1590-vers 1630)', in N. Jacques-Chaquin & M. Préaud (edd.): *Le sabbat des sorciers* q.v. 213-225

Walker Bynum C.: 'Religious women in the later Middle Ages', in J. Raitt (ed.): *Christian Spirituality*, Vol. 2: *High Middle Ages and Reformation* (SCM Press, New York 1988), 121-139

Westerkamp M.J.: *Women and Religion in Early America, 1600-1850*, (Routledge, London 1999)

Wilson E.: 'Institoris at Innsbruck: Heinrich Institoris, the Summis Desiderantes, and the Brixen Witch-Trial of 1485', in R. Scribner & T. Johnson (edd.): *Popular Religion in Germany and Central Europe, 1400-1800* (Macmillan 1996)

Wiltenburg J.: *Disorderly Women and Female Power in the Street Literature of Early Modern England and Germany* (University Press of Virginia 1992)

Winn Carlson C.: *A Fever in Salem* (Dee, Chicago 1999)

Wolpert W.: 'Fünfhundert Jahre Kreuzweg in Ediger an der Mosel. Inquisitor Institoris als Initiator', in G. Franz, F. Irsigler, E. Biesel (edd.): *Hexenglaube und Hexenprozesse im Raum Rhien-Mosel-Saar* (Spee, Trier 1996), 19-34

Wright R.M.: *Art and Antichrist in medieval Europe* (Manchester University Press 1995)

Trying a Witch

Boudreau L.C.: *Hans Baldung Grien and Albrecht Dürer: A Problem in Northern Mannerism*, PhD thesis, University of North Carolina, 1978

Briggs R.: *Witches and Neighbours* (Harper Collins, London 1996)

Gibson M.: *Reading Witchcraft* (Routledge, London 1999)

Maxwell-Stuart P.G. (ed.): *Martín del Rio, Investigations into Magic*, (Manchester University Press 2000)

—: *Witchcraft in Europe and the New World, 1400-1800* (Palgrave, London 2000)

Nurse J.: 'She-devils, harlots and harridans in Northern Renaissance prints', *History Today* 48 (July 1998), 41-48

Purkiss D.: *The Witch in History* (Routledge, London 1996)

Schild W.: 'Hexen-Bilder', in H. Eiden & R. Voltmer (edd.): *Methoden und Konzepte der historischen Hexenforschung* (Spee, Trier 1998)

Sharpe J.: *Instruments of Darkness: Witchcraft in England, 1550-1750* (Hamish Hamilton, London 1996)

—: *The Bewitching of Anne Gunter* (Profile Books, London 1999)

Strobino S.: *Françoise sauvée des flammes?* (Lausanne 1996)

Wiesner M.E.: *Women and Gender in Early Modern Europe* (Cambridge University Press 1993)

Zika C.:'Les parties du corps, Saturne et le cannibalisme: représentations
   visuelles des assemblées des sorcières au xvie siècle', in N. Jaques-Chaquin &
   M. Préaud (edd.): *Le sabbat des sorciers en Europe* (Grenoble 1993), 389-418
—:'Dürer's witch, riding women and moral order', in D. Eichberger & C. Zika
   (edd.): *Dürer and his Culture* (Cambridge University Press 1998), 118-140

Neither Gone Nor Forgotten

Ankarloo B. & Clark S. (edd.): *The Athlone History of Witchcraft and Magic*, Vol. 5:
   The Eighteenth and Nineteenth Centuries (Athlone Press, London 1999)
Bechtel G.: *La sorcière et l'Occident* (Plon, Paris 1997)
Behringer W.: Hexen: *Glaube, Verfolgung, Vermarktung* (Beck, Munich 1998)
Bostridge I.: *Witchcraft and its Transformations, c. 1650-c. 1750* (Clarendon, Oxford
   1997)
Briggs R.: *Witches and Neighbours* (Harper Collins, London 1996)
Clark S.: *Thinking With Demons* (Clarendon, Oxford 1999)
Clery E.J.: *The Rise of Supernatural Fiction, 1762-1800* (Cambridge University
   Press 1995)
Davies O.: *A People Bewitched: Witchcraft and Magic in Nineteenth-Century
   Somerset* (Bruton 1999)
—:'Cunning-folk in England and Wales during the eighteenth and nineteenth
   centuries', *Rural History* 8 (1997), 91-107
—:'Methodism, the clergy, and the popular belief in witchcraft and magic',
   History 82 (1997), 252-265
—:'Newspapers and the popular belief in witchcraft and magic in the modern
   period', *Journal of British Studies* 37 (1998), 136-165
—:'Urbanization and the decline of witchcraft: an examination of London',
   Journal of Social History 30 (1997), 597-617
—: *Witchcraft, Magic and Culture, 1736-1951* (Manchester University Press 1999)
Dillinger J., Fritz T., Mährle W. (edd.): *Zum Feuer verdammt: Die
   Hexenverfolgungen in der Grafschaft Hohenberg, der Reichstadt Reutlingen und der
   Fürstpropstei Ellwangen* (Steiner, Stuttgart 1998)
Dupont-Bouchat M.S.:'Le diable apprivoisé: la sorcellerie revisitée: magie et
   sorcellerie au xixe siècle', in R. Muchembled (ed.) Magie et Sorcellerie q.v.
   235-266
Estes L.L.:'Reginald Scot and his Discoverie of Witchcraft: religion and science
   in opposition to the European witch craze', *Church History* 52 (1983), 444-456
Flaherty G.: *Shamanism and the Eighteenth Century* (Princeton University Press
   1992)
Gijswijt-Hofstra M.:'Witchcraft after the witch-trials', in B. Ankarloo & S.
   Clark (edd.) *The Athlone History of Witchcraft and Magic*, q.v. 5. 97-189
Guskin P.J.:'The context of witchcraft: the case of Jane Wenham (1712)',
   Eighteenth Century Studies 15 (1981-2), 48-71

Harris R.: *Lourdes: Body and Spirit in the Secular Age* (Penguin, London 1999)

Hunter M.: 'Science and heterodoxy: an early modern problem reconsidered', in D.C. Lindberg & R.S. Westman (edd.): *Reappraisals of the Scientific Revolution* (Cambridge University Press 1990), 437-460

Hunter M. & Wootton D.: *Atheism from the Reformation to the Enlightenment*, (Clarendon, Oxford 1992)

Levack B.P.: 'The decline and end of witchcraft prosecutions', in B. Ankarloo & S. Clark (edd.): *The Athlone History of Witchcraft and Magic*, q.v. 5.1-93

Maxwell-Stuart P.G.: *Witchcraft in Europe and the New World, 1400-1800*, (Palgrave, London 2000)

Mossiker F.: *The Affair of the Poisons* (Victor Gollancz, London 1970)

Oldridge D.: 'Protestant conceptions of the Devil in early Stuart England', *History* 278 (2000), 232-246

Pohl H.: *Zauberglaube und Hexengast im Kurfürstentum Mainz* (Steiner, Stuttgart 1998)

Porter R.: 'Witchcraft and magic in Enlightenment, Romantic, and liberal thought', in B. Ankarloo & S. Clark (edd.): *The Athlone History of Witchcraft and Magic*, q.v. 5.193-282

Puhle A.: 'Ghosts, apparitions and poltergeist incidents in Germany between 1700 and 1900', *Journal of the Society for Psychical Research* 63 (1999), 292-305

Ramsay M.: *Professional and Popular Medicine in France, 1770-1830*, (Cambridge University Press 1988)

Sharp L.L.: 'Fighting for the afterlife: Spiritists, Catholics, and popular religion in nineteenth-century France', *Journal of Religious History* 23 (1999), 282-295

Sharpe J.: *The Bewitching of Anne Gunter* (Profile Books, London 1999)

Tourney G.: 'The physician and witchcraft in Restoration England', *Medical History* 16 (1972), 143-155

Walz R.: *Hexenglaube und magische Kommunikation im Dorf der Frühen Neuzeit* (Schöningh, Paderborn 1993)

The Modern Witch

Ankarloo B. & Clark S. (edd.): *The Athlone History of Witchcraft and Magic*: Vol. 6, *The Twentieth Century* (Athlone Press, London 1999)

Anon: *The Occult Census, 1989* (Sorcerer's Apprentice Press, Leeds 1989)

Blécourt W. de: 'The witch, her victim, the unwitcher, and the researcher: the continued existence of traditional witchcraft', in B. Ankarloo & S. Clark (edd.): *The Athlone History of Witchcraft and Magic*, Vol. 6 q.v. 143-219

Blum R. & Blum E: *Health and Healing in Rural Greece: A Study of Three Communities* (Stanford University Press 1965)

Compton C. & Cole G.: *Superstition* (Ebury Press, London 1990)

Davies O.: *Witchcraft, Magic and Culture, 1736-1951* (Manchester University Press 1999)

Drury N.: *Pan's Daughter: The Magical World of Rosaleen Norton* (Mandrake, Oxford 1988)

Dundes A. (ed.): *The Evil Eye: A Folklore Casebook* (Garland Publishing, London 1981)

Farrar J. & Farrar S.: *The Witches' Way* (Robert Hale, London 1984)

Favret-Saada J.: *Deadly Words: Witchcraft in the Bocage* (Cambridge University Press 1980)

Hutton R.: 'Modern pagan witchcraft', in B. Ankarloo & S. Clark (edd.): *The Athlone History of Witchcraft and Magic*, Vol. 6 q.v. 3–79

—: 'Paganism and polemic: the debate over the origins of modern pagan witchcraft', *Folklore* 111 (April 2000)

—: *The Triumph of the Moon* (Oxford University Press 1999)

Julliard A: 'Le malheur des sorts: sorcellerie d'aujourd'hui en France', in R. Muchembled (ed.): *Magie et Sorcellerie* q.v. 267–320

Lewis J.R. (ed.): *Magical Religion and Modern Witchcraft* (State University of New York 1996)

Luhrmann T.: *Persuasions of the Witch's Craft* (Blackwell, Oxford 1989)

Maloney C. (ed.): *The Evil Eye* (Columbia University Press 1976)

Miglione S.: *Mal'uocchiu: Ambiguity, Evil Eye, and the Language of Distress*, (University of Toronto 1997)

Muchembled R. (ed.): *Magie et Sorcellerie en Europe du Moyen Age à nos jours* (Armand Colin, Paris 1994)

Siebers T.: *The Mirror of Medusa* (University of California 1983)

LIST OF ILLUSTRATIONS

INDEX

DARK HISTORIES

A series of books exploring the darker
recesses of human history.

SERIES EDITOR

William Naphy, Senior Lecturer and
Head of History at the University of Aberdeen

PUBLISHED

P.G. Maxwell-Stuart, *Witchcraft: A History*
'Combines scholarly rigour with literary flair'
The Independent on Sunday

William Naphy & Andrew Spicer, *Plague*
'A chilling warning from history'
The Sunday Telegraph

William Naphy, *Sex Crimes*
'A model mix of of pin-sharp
scholarship and deep empathy'
The Guardian

COMMISSIONED

P. G. Maxwell-Stuart, *Wizards: A History*

Further titles are in preparation.